Simply
TRUFFLES

◆ PATRICIA WELLS ◆

Salad as a Meal

We've Always Had Paris . . . and Provence (with Walter Wells)

Vegetable Harvest

The Provence Cookbook

The Paris Cookbook

L'Atelier of Jöel Robuchon

Patricia Wells at Home in Provence

Patricia Wells' Trattoria

Simply French

Bistro Cooking

The Food Lover's Guide to France

The Food Lover's Guide to Paris

Simply TRUFFLES

RECIPES AND STORIES THAT CAPTURE
THE ESSENCE OF THE BLACK DIAMOND

· ·

PATRICIA WELLS

· ·

◆ *Photographs by* **JEFF KAUCK** ◆

WM

WILLIAM MORROW

An Imprint of HarperCollins*Publishers*

HarperCollins books may be purchased for educational, business, or sales promotional use. For information please write: Special Markets Department, HarperCollins Publishers, 10 East 53rd Street, New York, NY 10022.

FIRST EDITION

Designed by Lorie Pagnozzi

Library of Congress Cataloging-in-Publication Data
Wells, Patricia.
Simply truffles : recipes and stories that capture the essence of the black diamond / Patricia Wells ; photographs by Jeff Kauck.—1st ed.
p. cm.
Includes index.
ISBN 978-0-06-191519-2
1. Cooking (Truffles). 2. Cookbooks. I. Title.
TX804. 5.W45 2011
641.3'58—dc22   2011011528

11   12   13   14   15   ID5 / QG   10   9   8   7   6   5   4   3   2   1

The Richerenches Saturday truffle market

Truffle sign, Richerenches

Contents

Foreword

JOËL ROBUCHON

When Patricia Wells asked me to write the foreword to *Simply Truffles*, I was delighted to say yes. But I had to ask myself who I was saying "yes" to. Was it Patricia Wells the food journalist? Or Patricia Wells the award-winning cookbook author? Or Patricia Wells the cook?

Patricia has distinguished herself as all three, and in a lot of other ways besides. I got to know the full range of her talents when Patricia and I worked together to produce two books: *Simply French* (1991) and *The Atelier of Joël Robuchon* (1996). As we worked on each volume, we crisscrossed France to track down sources for the finest and freshest ingredients. Although we had already worked together in the compact kitchen at Jamin, my Paris restaurant at the time, I did not truly have the pleasure of sampling her cuisine until my wife and I were guests in Patricia and Walter's farmhouse in Provence. The fans of her cookbooks already knew that her cooking was accomplished and justly famous. As a guest *chez elle* in Provence, I learned that too.

Along with appreciating Patricia's talents as a cook, I also value her character and personality. She's never visibly stressed and always steady, and her desire to learn can flip to something approaching manic concentration as she focuses on understanding everything about a preparation in order to re-create it and give it her stamp.

I always say that passing along what I know is essential for me, and with Patricia, I had the feeling that when I taught she really got it—to the point that she could have easily passed the written exam to become one of the best chefs.

Luckily endowed with a limitless curiosity and insatiable appetite for discovery, Patricia knows how to make gastronomy an *art de vivre* for every day. Her talents as a writer allow her to evangelize for the cause, saving thousands of her readers and students at her cooking classes from the banal and the quotidian as their daily fare.

Charmed as she was by France, and especially in love with Provence, with a specialist's knowledge of the regional products, Patricia could not skip over the most exceptional product of the Provençal soil. When we first visited her in Provence, she had already delved into the world of the black truffle. Once there, we cooked with the magical mushroom and organized a trip to Richerenches, one of the best and most mysterious regional truffle markets, to dig for truffles with a producer in the region.

"The black diamond," as the *truffe melanosporum* or black French truffle is known, is one of the ingredients that has most influenced my dishes. It is in fact the ingredient that my clients appreciate the most.

Simple and delicious, it is best when combined with products that can best mate with its powerful taste and its absolutely unique perfume. Examples are the potato, eggs, and pasta. Or simply shave it raw in a salad, because with a truffle, it's the texture that matters—its crunchiness. It is a unique product that should be used as the *ingrédient d'honneur* in a dish and not just as décor on a plate.

Rare and delicate, the truffle should be used with subtlety, and as always Patricia "gets it." What we discover in this beautiful book is an array of original and tasty recipes. Patricia Wells, charming and talented ambassador for the truffle, succeeds beautifully in sharing her love for this mysterious product of incomparable taste.

JOËL ROBUCHON
PARIS, SPRING 2011

Preface

I don't remember the first time I encountered a truffle. And that's probably because it was unmemorable. For most of us, the first truffle experience comes in the form of a black speck in a slice of foie gras or as a tasteless, overcooked disk floating in a bowl of soup. And we say to ourselves, almost in relief, "Just another rare and expensive ingredient I don't have to care about." We put it on the "life list" and forget it.

But I do remember the first time I got excited about truffles and began to understand and appreciate their exceptional qualities. During the early 1980s I spent a lot of time in the kitchens of Parisian chef Joël Robuchon, where fresh black truffles were used in profusion. Robuchon was one of the first modern chefs to expand the traditional truffle repertoire, moving from heavy, rigid classics to lighter, modern, more inventive fare. I watched in awe as the chefs treated each black diamond with the utmost respect, peeling the firm outer rind or skin (the *peridium*) and mincing it into a fine dice to use as a simple garnish. The rest of the truffle (the flesh or pulp, the *gleba*) was thinly sliced on a mandoline, to use as a full-flavored garnish for his famous onion and bacon tartlets infused with the penetrating aroma and signature crunch of the truffle; in the fragrant warm salad of lamb's lettuce and potatoes; as well as in the unforgettable starter, a dome of pristine radicchio covered with a halo of revered black truffle slices.

When my husband, Walter, and I acquired a home in Provence in 1984, most Saturday mornings we took the high-speed train from Paris to Montélimar. On our way home from the train station, we drove through the village of Richerenches, passing this tiny village of 691 inhabitants around noon. Every winter weekend we witnessed the same scene: crowds of ruddy-faced beret-bearing farmers milling around, and groups gathered in clandestine-seeming poses, peering into the trunks of cars. As we rolled down the car windows for a better view, we found the air filled with a heady, wonderful, aromatic scent. After many months of this same strange scene, we realized that we were passing through one of France's largest truffle markets. Even though we never, ever, saw a single truffle.

At about the same time, truffle wars began on our property. Hand-painted signs reading *Défense de Truffé* appeared, as one local after another claimed rights to the truffles growing at the roots of the oak trees that border our vineyard. Yves, who had grown up on the property, still felt it was his land. We soon learned that we'd bought the property but didn't truly own it! Every person who had ever picnicked or hunted mushrooms on the land felt it was theirs. When we were away for stretches of time, we knew the poachers went wild. And when we arrived on weekends, farmers would appear seemingly out of nowhere, offering us "our share" of the hunt, usually a few tiny but precious black truffles.

In 1984 we also discovered Guy and Tina Jullien at their roadside hotel/restaurant La Beaugravière in Mondragon, about an hour's drive from our farmhouse. I remember our first visit, on a dramatically gusty, mistral-swept evening, when the winds nearly prevented us from making the short trip from the parking lot to the restaurant. We ate in the somber dining room that still sported 1930s oak tables and chairs, remnants of the pre-autoroute days when Beaugravière served as a stopping-off place for travelers coming from the north, heading for the Côte d'Azur. That evening we feasted on a giant truffle omelet, opulently studded with fragrant, fresh black truffles, paired with sips of local Rhône wine. (To this day, the truffle omelet, along with truffled scrambled eggs prepared with ultra-fresh farm eggs and a healthy dose of butter, remain two of the ten best ways to learn to appreciate the talents of the mysterious mushroom. We continue to return to the Julliens' modest restaurant, where truffle feasts await each winter.)

Soon, from November to March, our winter lives were filled with truffle lore. One year a bandit stole a bulldozer in the middle of the night, drove it down the country roads, and bulldozed one of the local truffle canneries, relieving the owners of the entire weekend's truffle purchases, about 100 kilos' worth, or 220 pounds of precious cargo. Another year thieves entered the same cannery on several occasions and grabbed as many canned truffles as they could get away with. One weekend we heard that one of the most important local truffle wholesalers had been "taken." The thieves climbed down his chimney in the middle of the night, gathered up the weekend's stash, and carried it away. And another time the local press reported that a wholesaler who had left the Saturday market in Richerenches with a trunkload of fresh truffles was held up at gunpoint as she entered her own home.

But for us, most of the drama has been in winter truffle hunts, truffle feasts, and truffle classes, as I have intensely explored the truffle and all its glories. The search is never ending. Here, then, I present more than twenty-five years of research and enjoyment. Share it with me.

PROVENCE

Introduction

Delicate, earthy, and increasingly rare, the prized black truffle—*Tuber melanosporum*—symbolizes the grand gastronomic glory of France, past and present. The writer Colette, who is said to have devoted one day each year to eating truffles, said it best: "If I can't have too many truffles, I'll do without truffles."

Although truffles have always been prized in France, their current rarity and price only add to the fanfare: In 1892, the French recorded a harvest of 2,200 tons of fresh truffles. Current annual yields come in at about 31 tons, with retail prices topping $2,000 a pound.

On some weekends at the truffle market in the Provençal village of Richerenches, more than 1 metric ton of the black fungus can change hands. (How much is that? One of the farmers told me recently that a ton would fill more than a cubic meter. That's about the size of the box that a washing machine comes in.) Found largely in France and in smaller quantities in Italy and Spain, truffles are harvested from November to March, reaching their peak flavor during the month of January.

There are more than 100 varieties of truffles, but only a few that are used in cooking. The best known are the winter black truffle (*Tuber melanosporum*); the summer "white" truffle, also known as *truffles de Saint Jean* (*Tuber aestivum*); Burgundy truffles (*Tuber uncinatum*); and Italian white truffles (*Tuber magnatum*). Summer truffles are delicious in their own right, but more common, less powerful, and about one twentieth the price of the winter truffle. The Burgundy truffle (misnamed, since it can be found in many countries in Europe) lies somewhere in between the summer truffle and the winter black truffle in intensity and flavor, and costs about one tenth the price of the *Tuber melanosporum*. Italian white winter truffles, also known as *truffes blanche d'Alba*, are softer and have a totally different color, texture, fragrance, and use than black truffles. They are even more rare and expensive than the French black truffle.

The truffle is among the world's most mysterious foods. Man has not tamed it, still has not figured out a surefire way to cultivate it, though progress is being made. Is its very elusiveness part of its charm? Perhaps what we *don't* know about the truffle is greater than what we do know.

In the triumvirate of luxury foods—caviar,

foie gras, and truffles—truffles turn out to be the eco good guy. While some kinds of caviar are banned on ecological grounds, and foie gras can be the subject of animal rights questions, truffles are simply a product of the soil. While a truffle is commonly considered a mushroom, it is more precisely a fungus closely related to mushrooms—the fruiting body of an underground fungus that grows in symbiosis with certain types of trees, mainly oak and hazelnut. Truffles are parasites that grow near the roots of the trees, 4 to 12 inches (10 to 30 centimeters) underground in stony, porous limestone-rich soil—although I have heard truffle farmers tell of finding them on top of the soil or just slightly hidden beneath a rock.

The truffle life cycle begins in March, when the spores germinate and begin to produce mycorrhiza, or fungus roots. In April, the fungus root colonizes the soil and produces more mycorrhiza. The fungus reaches sexual maturity in May, and by June the truffle is formed. It continues to grow slowly in July, more quickly in August, and more slowly again in September, and it reaches maturity in October. By late

November it is potentially ripe and ready to be unearthed. Harvesting continues through the end of February, and come March, the cycle starts anew.

In appearance a truffle is a rather inelegant, wrinkled black nugget generally the size of a walnut shell, although it can be as small as a pea and as large as an apple or orange. The mature truffle is firm, has wartlike bumps, and is a clean jet-black color. The flesh is black with distinctive white veins. (When a truffle is cooked or frozen, the white veiny matter turns to a clear liquid, which is why a fresh truffle has a better texture and more flavor than one that has been frozen or preserved.)

Climatic conditions are very important. The best hope is for alternating periods of sun and rain in March and April. Heavy rains in August help nourish the truffles when they are beginning to grow; in fact, most experts like to say that the truffle is "made" in the month of August. Truffles thrive on a rainy autumn, and their presence can sometimes be spotted by the burned patch (*brûlée*) around the base of the tree—the truffle's way of ensuring enough air for itself by killing the

undergrowth—or by the presence of a swarm of nearly invisible truffle flies that hover above the spot where the tuber is growing. They also grow best in limestone-rich soil and geographically, between the 40th and 47th parallels. (The village of Richerenches is at the 44th parallel.) Truffles tolerate neither deep winter freezes nor extremely dry summers.

A fungus with a capricious personality, its flavor is just as elusive. The subtle but powerful aroma of a fresh truffle is truly distinctive. It is earthy, with the scent of freshly turned soil

or autumnal woods, and with hints of other mushroom varieties. Many adjectives have been used to describe the black diamond: erotic, sexy, smoldering, penetrating, intense. As with many highly aromatic foods, it's the truffle's rich, pungent, and pervasive aroma that makes its flavor so singular. To the nose, the perfume of a truffle resembles a dry mushroom, humus, and wet forests. In the mouth, it has a distinctive crunch, with an earthy hazelnut flavor as well as a touch of bitterness. In chunks, it can take on an intense and overwhelming metallic taste, or even carry overtones of petroleum. The truffle is made up of 73 percent water, losing 5 percent of its weight each day in evaporation.

Today 80 percent of fresh French black truffles come from Provence (with markets in Richerenches, Carpentras, and Aups) and the rest from southwest of France (with markets in the towns of Sarlat, Sainte Alvère, and Lalbenque). Because of the truffle's longtime association with the southwest, it is often called *truffe du Périgord*, though today nearly all are found in the Vaucluse *département* of Provence.

We know a bit more about truffles today than they did in Roman times (when people believed the truffle was born of thunder or lightning and was used to eradicate demons), but not everything. Truffles are enveloped in secrecy: Even today much of the trading of truffles—changing hands from the farmers to brokers or (often unwary) individuals and always paid for in cash—is done out of open car trunks, laden with pillowcases bulging with truffles. In the wholesale markets there's no action and little to observe except groups of people standing around talking conspiratorially. It is no surprise that much folklore abounds, and even those savvy enough to know the difference between fact and fiction cling to the folklore as a matter of course. (One truffle farmer insisted to me—and by taking me on a tour of his truffle plantation, proved—that oak trees that produce round acorns produce perfectly round (and the most desirable) truffles, while oak trees that produce oval acorns produce oval, and less desirable, truffles.

Traditionally, farmers have saved the acorns from the most productive trees, planting them to produce new—and hopefully successful—truffle-producing offshoots. Yet even in a successful truffle plantation of oak trees, only a small percentage (some say 4 percent!) of the trees regularly produce truffles. Since 1997, farmers have had minimal—yet critical—success in planting trees that have been inoculated with truffle spores, a process called *mycorrhization.* Currently about 15 percent of the inoculated trees have been encouraged to produce truffles, and experts hope for greater success as experience and expertise in the field grows.

Part of the reason for the rarity of truffles is simple history. When vineyards in France were ravaged during the phylloxera epidemic of the 1860s, farmers in the south and southwest turned to truffle plantations as a potential source of income. Oak trees were planted and the huge truffle-producing years of the early part of the twentieth century seemed to prove the farmers right. Then World Wars I and II interrupted the pace: As soldiers went off to war, there was no one to till the soil in the truffle plantations. The truffle crop was reduced, and to this day it has never fully recovered.

While pigs traditionally have been used to sniff out the fragrant fungus, dogs have become

more common. There are two reasons: Pigs root to live, not to amuse their owners, and they often ingest the truffle before the master can pry it loose. Also, since poaching is a common practice, as the story goes, if you put a pig in the back seat of your car, it might attract attention—but a dog will hardly be noticed. While no particular breed of dog is used most often, most truffle-hunting dogs are females (because of their heightened sense of smell) and usually of mixed breed. Their folkloric names—Anda, Pamela, Dynamo, Penelope, and even Lassie and Come On—help enrich the story, as do their various personalities. Some dogs attack their job with flair, racing through the truffle plantation like cartoon characters and screeching to a stop when the truffle fragrance rises from the soil. They will dig furiously, being careful to unearth, but not harm, the prized truffle. Other dogs play it cool, prancing slowly, tapping the soil with nonchalance, nodding to their master, and waiting impatiently for their treat—usually a piece of sausage or a cookie. I have even seen dogs dig up truffles and carry them daintily in their mouth like a retriever, delivering them to their master unharmed! A well-trained truffle dog not only knows how to unearth a truffle but can tell by the scent whether a truffle is "ripe" and ready to be harvested. And what happens if a ripe truffle is never unearthed? Like an unharvested mushroom, it simply decomposes and become part of the soil.

When truffles are unearthed, they are covered with soil. A fresh black truffle is firmer than any other mushroom, and the soil is removed with a stiff brush and plenty of cold running water. (In fact, professional truffle wholesalers soak the truffles in water and store them in a chilled room before actually brushing off the dirt.)

Once you are home from the hunt or the market, what are the best ways to extract maximum advantage from this knobby little jewel? Truffles need to be teased, coaxed, and left in contact with ingredients for a certain amount of time to exhale their intense fragrance. The truffle's best friends include cheese, butter, cream, all mushrooms, pasta, rice, potatoes, artichokes, Jerusalem artichokes, pumpkin, celery root, and chestnuts. Oysters, salmon, scallops, and poultry are good companions, but to my mind meats do nothing to enhance a truffle.

A truffle hunt, near Puymeras in Provence

And while many chefs work truffles into desserts—I have made and sampled truffle ice cream, sorbets, and panna cotta—I find I prefer to enjoy my truffles in savories.

If carefully stored in an airtight container in the refrigerator, a fresh truffle will last up to one week, losing about 5 percent of its weight by evaporation each day after it is unearthed. Because truffles are expensive as well as elusive, cooks should do all they can to charm them into sharing their dramatic aroma and flavor. One-third ounce (10 grams) of truffle per person is considered a generous dose for an omelet, pasta, risotto, or polenta. An average truffle—about the size of a golf ball—weighs about 1 ounce (30 grams) and will yield twenty to twenty-five thin slices.

Once a cleaned fresh truffle reaches your kitchen, here are some suggestions:

- Place the truffle in a glass jar with several fresh eggs in their shells (preferably organic and free range), and secure tightly. Use the eggs in omelets, crepes, risotto, pasta, or poached atop polenta.

- While not all cooks peel truffles, I do. The exterior "skin," called the *peridium*, has a firmer texture. I find that texture advantageous, for when it is peeled and minced, it adds crunch to homemade truffle salt, butter, and cream.

Black truffles are best if never really cooked, per se. One can wrap a whole truffle in parchment paper and foil and warm it in a bed of wood cinders, but that's not cooking it; it's simply a way to release the juices and soften the truffle. For maximum flavor and texture, cut truffles in thin, elegant slices or in thicker matchsticks and add them to warm food at the last moment. This is when the truffle gives the best expression of itself, in both aroma and flavor. The crunch of the truffle is essential to its enjoyment and appreciation.

After years of tasting and experimenting, I've concluded that man has not been able to capture the essence of the truffle artificially. Virtually all truffle products—oils, mustards, creams, pastas, butters, polentas, and risottos—have been infused with truffle "essence," basically a chemical (think perfume) whose flavor and aroma are overtly intense and thoroughly objectionable. I'll disagree with Colette here: I'd rather have a small amount of truffle than anything infused with truffle essence! Better to prepare your own salt, butters, and cream, infusing them with the flavor of true fresh minced truffles.

WHAT ATTRACTS AN ANIMAL TO A TRUFFLE IN THE FIRST PLACE?

All truffles—to a lesser or greater degree—secrete a substance called *pheromone*, a chemical that is also secreted in the testicles and saliva of the male pig, wild boar, men's armpits, women's urine, and some members of the cabbage family. The substance is secreted by truffles as a means of spreading their spores but also serves to attract animals to unearth them.

WHAT IS THE BEST WAY TO CONSERVE A TRUFFLE?

During the truffle season, from late November to early March, professional truffle suppliers buy up fresh truffles, clean them, pack them in vacuum-sealed bags, and then ship them around the world in refrigerated containers. If there is an excess of truffles, the truffles are sterilized in large tin cans. Then, in the off season, the tins are opened and the truffles are sized and placed in small glass jars or tins and sterilized once more. The liquid from the first sterilization is then canned as truffle juice, an excellent ingredient, one that offers incredible truffle flavor for less money than a fresh truffle.

At home, a fresh truffle can be stored in an airtight container in the refrigerator for up to 1 week. I store mine in a jar with whole eggs in their shells. The truffle permeates the eggshell and infuses the eggs with an exhilarating aroma and flavor. (One Christmas we left Provence, returning to Paris for just a few days. I had a huge jar of eggs and truffles in the refrigerator and decided to take just the truffles back to the city; the eggs remained in the refrigerator in the jar. Upon our return, I opened the refrigerator and was welcomed with the familiar, penetrating aroma. We made scrambled eggs that day, and didn't need a single truffle to enjoy the pure truffle essence in our dinner.)

HOW MUCH TRUFFLE DOES ONE NEED FOR A TRUE TRUFFLE EXPERIENCE?

Traditionally, about 1/3 ounce (or 10 grams) of truffle per person is considered generous, especially when added to eggs, potatoes, pasta, polenta, and grains. A single 1/2-ounce (15-gram) truffle will yield about 20 thin slices, and the peelings will yield 1 tablespoon (6 grams) of minced truffle to use to prepare truffle salt, cream, or butter. Flavor can be enhanced and boosted tremendously by additionally seasoning the dish with store-bought truffle juice or with homemade truffle salt, truffle butter, or truffle cream. Sometimes I use all four in a dish.

IS THERE A DIFFERENCE IN QUALITY AND FLAVOR BETWEEN A "WILD" TRUFFLE AND A "CULTIVATED" TRUFFLE?

The experts say no, that a truffle is a truffle. Today 80 percent of the truffles found in France come from trees that have been successfully inoculated with the truffle spores, a technique called *mycorrhization* that has been used since

1997 with varied success. Experts say that the inoculation works about 15 percent of the time. Each year in France, Spain, and Italy, farmers are now planting about 247,000 acres (100,000 hectares) in hopes of continued successful harvests.

WHAT IS THE DIFFERENCE BETWEEN FRESH TRUFFLES, FROZEN TRUFFLES, CANNED TRUFFLES, AND TRUFFLE JUICE?

Fresh, frozen, and canned truffles can be used interchangeably. Obviously, fresh is best, for the fresh truffle offers the best flavor and texture. Frozen and canned truffles lose much of the prized texture and crunch, but they are still worthy substitutes. Truffle juice is the pure liquid that comes from the truffle when it is preserved. Generally, truffles are preserved in large quantities in large tins. The tins are then reopened, the juice is reserved for canning as truffle juice, and the whole truffles are put into jars or tins and preserved once again. Truffle juice can be used to boost the flavor (or even replace the truffle) in many dishes. When I open a can of truffle juice, I use what I need that day and freeze the rest in small containers. A little goes a long way. Do not try to reduce the juice itself: it contains salt and will become overly salty.

IF I HAVE NO TRUFFLES, CAN I STILL USE THE RECIPES IN THIS BOOK?

All the recipes in this book stand on their own, delicious with or without truffles. In most cases the truffle is a last-minute embellishment. Fresh or rehydrated wild mushrooms, particularly morels, may be added in place of truffles.

Truffle Time Line

2000 BC   The first known text about the truffle is recorded by the Neo-Sumerians on clay tablets.

500 BC   An alien resident of Athens is given citizenship as a reward for inventing a new way to prepare truffles.

300 BC   The truffle appears in *A History of Plants*, the work of Greek philosopher Theophrastus.

AD 400   The oldest surviving truffle recipes can be found in the first known European cookbook, *Apicius,* which records cooking and dining in Imperial Rome. Included are six recipes for cooking truffles, a recipe for wine sauce made with truffles, and methods of storing truffles in sawdust. The author is believed to be Marcus Gavius Apicius, a celebrated gourmand who lived during the reign of Augustus and Tiberius.

AD 350–500   Truffles acquire a sinister reputation during the Dark Ages; they are considered a sign of the presence of the devil and believed to be grown from the spit of witches. During the Holy Inquisition, the truffle is described as "black as the soul of the damned" and banned from the kitchen because of it seductive appeal.

AD 1000   Truffles are featured in the medical writings of the Persian physician Avicenna (considered the forefather of modern medicine) as a treatment for healing wounds, weakness, vomiting, and pain. The variety of truffle he wrote about, the *Terfezia* or desert truffle, is now known to contain antibiotics.

AD 1100	The Carpentras truffle market is established in Provence, and is still held every Friday morning from November to March. In 1155 Raymond V, Count of Toulouse, insists on its exclusivity and bans the creation of all other markets between the Ouvèze and Sorgue rivers.
AD 1316	Pope John XXII is installed in Avignon and plants oak trees nearby in hopes that truffles will follow.
AD 1500	A sixteenth-century travel writer describes the sight of twenty-five or thirty camels laden down with truffles being transported from the mountains of Armenia and Turkey, where they were grown, to the market in Damascus. A love for truffles in the region traces back to ancient Babylonia, where they were bountiful along the banks of the Euphrates and Tigris rivers.
AD 1526	French king François I discovers the black truffle during his capture in Madrid and reintroduces it to France upon his return, serving mounds of them at sumptuous banquets at the court in Fontainebleau.
AD 1533	Catherine de Médicis introduces the white truffle (*Tuber magnatum*) to France.
AD 1651	François Pierre de la Varenne includes more than sixty truffle recipes in *Le Cuisinier François,* the founding text of modern French cuisine, and is the first chef known to pair truffles with foie gras.
AD 1808	The beginnings of the golden age of truffles: Joseph Talon (from the French village of Saint-Saturnin-lès-Apt in Provence) creates the first cultivated *truffière,* or truffle plantation, by planting acorns from oak trees that were already known to produce truffles. He had success and soon becomes the largest truffle producer in the region. He is, of course, widely copied.

AD 1810 A Frenchman, Nicolas Appert (1749–1841), creates a canning method that allows for the conservation of all manner of foods, including truffles, thus preserving their flavor and perfume. Napoléon Bonaparte had offered an award of 12,000 francs to the person who could invent a useful way of preserving food for his army. After fifteen years of experimentation, Appert succeeded—nearly 100 years after Louis Pasteur proved that heat killed bacteria. Appert's method was to fill thick, large-mouthed bottles with foods of every description, ranging from beef, poultry, eggs, and milk to prepared dishes. He left air space at the top of the bottle and sealed it with a cork and a metal vise. The bottle was wrapped in canvas to protect it, then cooked in boiling water. To this day, canned French truffles and truffle juice may note on their label *"Extrait par Appertisation"* (Extracted by the Appert Method).

AD 1847 August Rousseau, a truffle grower in Carpentras, plants seventeen acres of oak trees from acorns gathered beneath truffle-producing oaks. His harvest is so large that he receives a prize at the 1855 World's Fair in Paris.

AD 1863 Vineyards in France are ravaged by a phylloxera epidemic. In a region where the land is favorable to truffle growth, oak trees replace vines, and intensive truffle production begins in earnest.

AD 1892 A record year for truffles in France: 2,200 tons (2,000 tonnes).

AD 1910 French truffle production declines to 1,100 tons (1,000 tonnes).

AD 1914 Truffle production suffers as World War I continues; truffle farms are abandoned and left unattended.

AD 1938 The first edition of the cookbook *Larousse Gastronomique* is published, with a recipe that begins "Take three pounds of truffles, the biggest you can find, round, smooth, firm, and very black."

AD 1940s	Truffle production continues to decline, to 410 tons (400 tonnes), as farmers concentrate on staple crops and more and more people move to the cities.
AD 1950s	Mechanized agriculture hardens the land and uproots truffles. Production falls to less than 10 tons (11 tonnes) in the worst years.
AD 1960	French truffle production increases to 132 tons (120 tonnes).
AD 1975	French chef Paul Bocuse creates his famous Black Truffle Soup V.G.E. for the Elysée Palace when presented with the Legion of Honor by President Valéry Giscard d'Estaing. The soup is a heady combination of black truffles, foie gras, and chicken, the bowl covered dramatically with puff pastry so you must dig your way into the soup, like a truffle hunter.
AD 1977	In France, the first truffle is unearthed beneath an artificially mychorrizalized tree (one inoculated with truffle spores). Subsequently a vast plantation movement is launched in France with hopes to revive truffle production. Today, about 80 percent of all truffles in France are found beneath trees that have been inoculated with truffle spores.
AD 1981	French chef Joël Robuchon opens his restaurant Jamin and soon offers an all-truffle menu that includes his famous Salad of Lamb's Lettuce, Potato, and Black Truffles; the Onion and Bacon and Truffle Tartelet; and Radicchio Salad covered with a generous mound of glistening truffles. He alters the way French chefs treat truffles, moving away from heavy, classic dishes and toward lighter, more modern fare.
AD 1985	French chef Guy Savoy creates his still-famous Artichoke Soup with Black Truffles, accompanied by a warm mushroom brioche spread with truffle butter.

AD 1985   French truffle production declines again, to 66 tons (60 tonnes).

AD 1987   Research chemists discover for the first time the aromatic constituents of the black truffle. Research shows that the black truffle exudes up to eighty components. Nine constituents are isolated, including dimethyl sulfate. This discovery makes it possible to create an artificial truffle aroma, available on the market today as scented truffle oil.

AD 1997   At the end of January, several truffle dogs are stolen in the village of Pernes-les-Fontaines, near Carpentras. Agence France Presse reports that the thieves were certainly locals, since they returned some dogs that had no talent for rooting out truffles.

AD 2010   Truffle production in France declines to 31 tons (30 tonnes), though with positive climatic conditions, the number could almost double.

TRUFFLE MENUS

A SUMMER TRUFFLE FEAST

Zucchini Blossoms Stuffed with Goat Cheese and Summer Truffles 161

Green Zebra Tomatoes with Parmesan and Summer Truffles 48

Creamy Polenta with Truffles and Poached Eggs 85

Truffled Saint-Marcellin 101

ANY TIME YOU HAVE A FEW TRUFFLES

A Potato Chip, a Truffle Slice 38

Pine Nut, Pancetta, Goat Cheese, and Truffle Salad 42

Goat Cheese Cannelloni with Morels and Truffles 114

Tête de Moine with Curried Walnuts and Truffles 109

A HOLIDAY FEAST WITH FRIENDS

Truffles Wrapped in Parchment and Warmed in Wood Cinders 159

Warm Oysters with Truffle Cream and Truffles 144

Seared Duck Breast with Truffled *Sauce Poulette* 150

Belgian Endive, Pine Nut, Chive, and Truffle Salad 45

CHEESE, SOUP, RISOTTO

Goat Cheese "Reverse Oreos" with Truffles 25

Artichoke Soup with Parmesan and Truffles 58

Truffle Risotto with Parmesan Broth 121

Truffled Vacherin du Mont d'Or 107

A NOVEMBER FESTIVAL

Truffled *Croque Monsieur* 30

Pumpkin Soup with Truffle Cream, Curry, Pumpkin Seed Oil, and Truffles 61

Seared Truffled Scallops with Coppa and Lamb's Lettuce Salad 147

PIZZA, POT-AU-FEU, AND SALAD

Pecorino-Romano and Truffle Pizza 174

Chicken Pot-au-Feu with Truffles 152

Truffle, Potato, and Watercress Salad 53

LET'S INVITE FRIENDS OVER

Open-Faced Truffle Sandwiches 28

Vito's Potato Soup with Parmesan Cream and Truffles 70

Six-Minute Steamed Salmon with Shellfish Cream and Truffles 142

WHAT TO DO WITH 2 OUNCES (60 GRAMS) OF TRUFFLES

You don't need to create a $1,000 roast chicken to explore and enjoy the pleasures of truffles. Here are two menus for two—I am thinking of quiet, romantic, intimate dinners—that can be created with a total just 2 ounces (60 grams) of fresh black truffles, or about two average-sized mushrooms.

First fill an airtight container with at least 4 large farm-fresh eggs in their shells (preferably organic and free range), add the 2 truffles, seal the container, and store in the refrigerator for at least 2 days and up to 1 week. Then:

1. Peel the truffles, mince the peelings, and store them in a small airtight container. Each truffle should yield about 1 tablespoon (6 grams) of minced peelings.

2. Prepare the Truffle Salt: Combine 1 tablespoon (6 grams) minced peelings with 1 tablespoon fine sea salt in a small jar, secure the lid, and shake to blend. (Store in the freezer up to 6 months, use as needed, no need to thaw.)

3. Prepare the Truffle Butter: Mash 1 tablespoon (6 grams) of minced peelings with 4 tablespoons (2 ounces; 60 grams) of softened butter. Store, covered, in the refrigerator for up to 3 days.

4. With a mandoline or a very sharp knife, slice each truffle into very thin rounds. A truffle should yield about 20 slices. Place the slices in a small jar, and tighten the lid. The slices can be used right away or stored, covered, in the refrigerator for up to 3 days.

INTIMATE TRUFFLE DINNERS FOR TWO

TRUFFLED *CROQUE MONSIEUR* (USING 2 SLICES OF BRIOCHE) 30

ARTICHOKE SOUP WITH PARMESAN AND TRUFFLES 58

SIX-MINUTE STEAMED SALMON WITH SHELLFISH CREAM AND TRUFFLES 142

TRUFFLED SAINT-MARCELLIN (ONE CHEESE) 101

OPEN-FACED TRUFFLE SANDWICHES (2 SANDWICHES) 28

SPAGHETTI WITH PARMESAN AND TRUFFLE BUTTER (HALF RECIPE) 119

PINE NUT, PANCETTA, GOAT CHEESE, AND TRUFFLE SALAD (HALF RECIPE) 42

OPENING ACTS

GOAT CHEESE "REVERSE OREOS" WITH TRUFFLES 25

OPEN-FACED TRUFFLE SANDWICHES 28

TRUFFLED *CROQUE MONSIEUR* 30

TRUFFLE AND MOZZARELLA *TARTINES* 33

FRESH COD *BRANDADE* WITH TRUFFLES 35

A POTATO CHIP, A TRUFFLE SLICE 38

GOAT CHEESE "REVERSE OREOS" WITH TRUFFLES

During my January Truffle Week class, this is often the first taste of truffle I offer students. As guests pass through the doors of our farmhouse kitchen, I offer them a few of these toasty warm, melted goat cheese appetizers. I call them "reverse Oreos" because a slice of fresh black truffle is layered between two slices of goat's milk cheese. During my latest class, this was voted "Best Taste of the Week," winning out over many more elaborate truffle creations.

20 SERVINGS

EQUIPMENT: *A small jar with a lid; a mandoline or a very sharp knife; unflavored dental floss or a very sharp knife; a 1 1/2-inch (3 cm) round pastry cutter; a baking sheet.*

1 fresh black truffle (about 1 ounce; 30 g), cleaned (see Note)

8 ounces (250 g) soft goat's milk cheese, in 1 1/2-inch (3 cm) cylinders

8 thin slices Brioche (page 178)

1 tablespoon (15 g) Truffle Butter (page 191)

Truffle Salt (page 186)

1. Arrange a rack in the oven about 3 inches (7.5 cm) from the heat source. Preheat the broiler.

2. With a vegetable peeler, peel the truffle. Mince the truffle peelings, place them in the jar, and tighten the lid. Reserve the peelings for another use. With the mandoline or very sharp knife, cut the truffle into very thin slices. The truffle should yield about 20 slices.

3. With the dental floss or very sharp knife, cut the cheese into rounds about 1/4 inch (5 mm) thick. The cheese should yield about 40 slices. Make "reverse Oreos" by placing a slice of cheese on a plate, topping it with a slice of truffle, and topping the truffle with another slice of cheese.

4. With the pastry cutter, cut the brioche into 20 rounds. Place the rounds side by side on a baking sheet. Butter them lightly. Place the baking sheet under the broiler and toast the brioche lightly. Remove from the oven and place the truffle "Oreos" on top of the toasted brioche rounds.

5. Return the baking sheet to the oven and broil just until the cheese is soft, 1 to 2 minutes. Remove from the oven and season lightly with the truffle salt. Serve immediately.

NOTE: *When purchased from professional suppliers, fresh truffles will generally be cleaned. When purchased direct from farmers, they will generally still be covered with soil. Scrub them thoroughly under cold running water to remove the soil.*

WINE SUGGESTION: *Both simple and elegant, these little bites go well with any mineral-rich wine. A favorite local white comes from the vineyards of Domaine des Escaravailles, where winemakers Gilles and Daniel Ferran make an assortment of exciting wines. A favorite white is their Côtes-du-Rhône Villages Rasteau La Galopine, a beautiful blend of Roussanne, Marsanne, and Viognier, aged gently in wood, offering a harmonious blend of acid and fruit and a light touch of minerality.*

"Let me put the case for treasuring the truffle. Leaving aside culinary considerations, the truffle is not just a fragrance, a flavor, a face—though all of these things contribute to its allure—it's a nugget of vegetable matter searching, as must all living things, for a niche in which it can thrive. And its niche is remarkably specific. Let one thing fall out of line, and the whole enterprise falters and fails."

—ELIZABETH LUARD,
TRUFFLES (2006)

OPEN-FACED TRUFFLE SANDWICHES

These appealing little sandwiches are one of the best ways to enjoy and experience a black truffle. Be sure to use the best brioche, real truffle butter, and real truffle salt. Life does not get better than this.

4 SERVINGS

EQUIPMENT: *A baking sheet.*

4 thin slices Brioche (page 178)

1 tablespoon (15 g) Truffle Butter (page 191)

16 fresh black truffle slices

Extra-virgin olive oil spray

Truffle Salt (page 186)

1. Arrange a rack in the oven about 3 inches (7.5 cm) from the heat source. Preheat the broiler.

2. Place the brioche slices side by side on the baking sheet. Spread with the truffle butter. Place the baking sheet under the broiler and toast the brioche lightly.

3. Arrange 4 truffle slices side by side on each slice of toasted brioche. Return the baking sheet to the broiler, and heat just until the truffles are slightly warmed, about 30 seconds. Remove from the oven. Spray lightly with the oil and season lightly with the salt. Serve immediately.

WINE SUGGESTION: *Champagne, and more Champagne. Break the bank and go for a real treasure, the offering from Egly-Ouriet Père et Fils. Their non-vintage* brut blanc de noirs grand cru *is made from old-vine pinot noir with a gentle touch of oak, a fine balance to the toastiness of the brioche and a worthy company for the fresh black truffle.*

A GOOD DAY'S HARVEST
In 1858, a property owner in Carpentras, Monsieur Rousseau, dug up, with the help of 4 pigs, 23 kilos (50 pounds) of truffles in 5 hours.

TRUFFLED *CROQUE MONSIEUR*

This "everyday" French sandwich with truffles was popularized by chef Michel Rostang and remains a part of his spectacular truffle menus each winter in Paris. I also sampled a more rustic—and equally spectacular—version of this opener at one of my favorite Paris restaurants, Bistrot Paul Bert, where owner Bertrand Auboyneau always surprises us with new and unexpected treats.

8 SERVINGS

EQUIPMENT: *A small jar with a lid; a mandoline or a very sharp knife.*

1 fresh black truffle (about 1 ounce; 30 g), cleaned (see Note, page 26)

8 thin slices Brioche (page 178)

1 tablespoon (15 g) Truffle Butter (page 191), at room temperature

1 tablespoon (15 g) Clarified Butter (recipe follows)

1 teaspoon extra-virgin olive oil

1. With a vegetable peeler, peel the truffle. Mince the truffle peelings, place them in the jar, and tighten the lid. Reserve the peelings for another use. With the mandoline or very sharp knife, cut the truffle into very thin slices. The truffle should yield about 20 slices.

2. Butter one side of each slice of brioche with the truffle butter. Arrange 4 slices of brioche, buttered side up, side by side on a platter. Arrange 4 or 5 truffle slices side by side on top of each slice of brioche. Place another slice of buttered brioche, buttered side down, on top of each layer of truffles, to make a sandwich. Wrap each sandwich tightly in plastic wrap. Refrigerate for at least 6 hours and up to 24 hours.

3. At serving time, in a large skillet, melt the clarified butter and oil over medium heat. Add the sandwiches, in batches if necessary, and brown the bread on both sides until golden, 1 to 2 minutes per side. Cut each *croque monsieur* in half. Serve immediately.

CLARIFIED BUTTER

What is clarified butter? And why bother? Clarified butter is butter that has the milk solids and water removed. This gives it a much higher smoking point than regular butter and lets you cook at a higher temperature without burning. Without the milk solids, clarified butter can also be kept fresher longer than non-clarified butter. I use it, often in conjunction with a touch of oil, when cooking foods that I want to sauté at a high heat without burning, such as the Truffled *Croque Monsieur*.

ABOUT 6 TABLESPOONS (3 OUNCES; 90 G)

EQUIPMENT: *A double boiler or a microwave oven; a fine-mesh sieve; dampened cheesecloth.*

8 tablespoons (4 ounces; 120 g) unsalted butter

1. *If you are using the double boiler,* cut the butter into small pieces and place them in the top of a double boiler set over simmering water. When the butter has melted, raise the heat to moderate and let the butter simmer until it stops crackling, an indication that the butter is beginning to "fry." Remove from the heat and let the residue settle to the bottom of the pan: there should be a layer of milk solids on the bottom and a layer of foam on top. *If you are using the microwave,* place the butter in a 1 1/2-quart (1.5 l) microwave-safe dish. (Do not use a smaller container or the butter will splatter all over the oven.) Cover loosely with paper towels. Microwave at full power for 2 1/2 minutes. Remove from the oven and let the residue settle to the bottom of the dish: there should be a layer of milk solids on the bottom and a layer of foam on top.

2. With a spoon, skim off and discard the top layer of foam. Line the sieve with the dampened cheesecloth, and slowly strain the melted butter into a container; discard the milky solids that remain. (Store in an airtight container in the refrigerator for up to 1 month.)

WINE SUGGESTION: *A medium-bodied white wine is in order here. While one could splurge on Château de Beaucastel's stunning Châteauneuf-du-Pape, we are never disappointed to sip the same winemaker's simple white Perrin & Fils Côtes-du-Rhône Réserve Blanc, a crisp, finely acidic, and refreshing blend of Viognier, Roussanne, and Grenache Blanc.*

"When I eat truffles, I become livelier, gayer, more amenable; inside me, especially in my veins, I feel a voluptuous, gentle warmth that soon communicates itself to my head."

—ALEXANDRE DUMAS, *GRAND DICTIONNAIRE DE CUISINE* (1873)

TRUFFLE AND MOZZARELLA *TARTINES*

Our winemaker, Yves Gras, raved about these totally obvious and supremely delicious little openers: truffles love fat, especially that from a soft cheese such as mozzarella, which seems to virtually suck up the intense truffle flavors, particularly when lightly warmed. These *tartines*, or open-faced sandwiches, have become truffle season favorites.

20 SERVINGS

EQUIPMENT: *A small jar with a lid; a mandoline or a very sharp knife; a 1 1/2-inch (3 cm) round pastry cutter; a baking sheet.*

1 fresh black truffle (about 1 ounce; 30 g), cleaned (see Note, page 26)

About 4 ounces (120 g) small mozzarella balls

8 thin slices Brioche (page 178)

1 tablespoon (15 g) Truffle Butter (page 191), at room temperature

1 teaspoon extra-virgin olive oil

Truffle Salt (page 186)

1. Arrange a rack in the oven about 3 inches (7.5 cm) from the heat source. Preheat the broiler.

2. With a vegetable peeler, peel the truffle. Mince the truffle peelings, place them in the jar, and tighten the lid. Reserve the peelings for another use. With the mandoline or very sharp knife, cut the truffle into very thin slices. The truffle should yield about 20 slices.

3. With a very sharp knife, cut the cheese into slices about ¼ inch (5 mm) thick. The cheese should yield about 20 slices.

4. With the pastry cutter, cut the brioche into 20 rounds. Place the rounds side by side on the baking sheet. Lightly butter the brioche. Place the baking sheet under the broiler and toast the brioche lightly. Remove the baking sheet from the oven and place the cheese slices on top of the toast.

5. Return the baking sheet to the oven and broil just until the cheese is soft, 1 to 2 minutes. Remove from the oven, place a truffle slice on top of the cheese, brush lightly with the oil, and sprinkle with a bit of the salt. Serve immediately.

WINE SUGGESTION: *Truffle and wine marriages are easy: a white Châteauneuf-du-Pape wins every time. Yes, it's rare and expensive, but when it comes to truffles, nothing is too good. A favorite is the offering from Château La Nerthe. Their special cuvée Clos de Beauvenir, made with almost 100 percent Roussanne grapes, is elegant, crisp, and full-flavored and has a forward minerality that marries perfectly with truffles.*

"To tell the story of the truffle is to tell the history of world civilization."

—ALEXANDRE DUMAS, *GRAND DICTIONNAIRE DE CUISINE* (1873)

FRESH COD *BRANDADE* WITH TRUFFLES

The smooth, almost smoky flavor of this fresh cod and potato puree teams up beautifully with the delicate crunch of a single slice of truffle. The contrast of the alabaster puree with the jet-black truffle adds a fine touch of drama. I serve these as openers: a gentle dollop set on a white porcelain spoon, pierced with a slice of truffle.

20 SERVINGS

EQUIPMENT: *A wire-mesh tea infuser; a fine-mesh sieve; a food processor.*

1 pound (500 g) skinned fresh cod, preferably Alaskan Pacific cod

8 ounces (250 g) yellow-fleshed potatoes (such as Yukon Gold), peeled

1 cup (250 ml) heavy cream

1 cup (250 ml) whole milk

5 plump, moist garlic cloves, peeled, halved, and green germ removed

1 imported bay leaf

2 sprigs fresh thyme

1 teaspoon whole white peppercorns

2 tablespoons coarse sea salt

3 tablespoons minced fresh flat-leaf parsley leaves

3 tablespoons minced fresh chives

Fine sea salt

20 fresh black truffle slices

1. Cut the cod and the potatoes into 1/2-inch (1.25 cm) cubes.

2. In a large saucepan, combine the cream, milk, and cod. Place the garlic, bay leaf, thyme, and peppercorns in the wire-mesh tea infuser and add it to the pan. Add the coarse salt. Bring the liquid just to a simmer over medium heat, and cook, uncovered, until the fish is cooked through, about 1 minute. Place the sieve over a bowl. With a slotted spoon, transfer the fish to the sieve. Leave the cooking liquid in the pan.

3. Place the potatoes in the cooking liquid used to poach the cod. Simmer, uncovered, over medium heat, stirring regularly, until a knife inserted into a potato comes away easily, about 15 minutes. Drain the potatoes. (Remove the tea infuser. The cooking liquid can be reserved for soups or sauces.)

4. Place the cod, potatoes, parsley, and chives in the food processor and puree. Taste for seasoning and add fine sea salt if needed. Place a dollop of *brandade* on a spoon. Stand a truffle slice on end in the *brandade*. Repeat for the remaining servings. Serve immediately.

WINE SUGGESTION: *Denis Alary, in the nearby village of Cairanne, makes some stunning white wines, and a favorite is their Vin de Pays La Grange Daniel, a 100 percent Roussanne that is well priced and goes down easily, a perfect opener to a fine meal.*

"The truffle is a positive aphrodisiac, and under certain circumstances makes women kinder, and men more amiable."

—JEAN-ANTHELME BRILLAT-SAVARIN, *THE PHYSIOLOGY OF TASTE* (1825)

A POTATO CHIP, A TRUFFLE SLICE

A fresh black truffle slice adores the company of a fresh potato chip. For sure it is attracted, like us, to the saltiness, the fat, the crunch. I adore serving this to a crowd. Is there anyone who does not love, perhaps even crave, potato chips? I have a tiny electric fryer that holds just 1 quart (1 l) of oil, making it handy for quick and easy frying. It is amazing how many chips one gets out of a single potato!

20 SERVINGS

EQUIPMENT: *A mandoline or a very sharp knife; an electric deep-fat fryer, fitted with a basket.*

One 8-ounce (250 g) yellow-fleshed potato (such as Yukon Gold), peeled

1 quart (1 l) vegetable oil (such as sunflower) for deep-fat frying (see Note)

Fine sea salt

20 fresh black truffle slices

1. With the mandoline or very sharp knife, slice the potato paper-thin. Wash the potato slices in warm water and drain thoroughly. Arrange the slices in a single layer on a large kitchen towel, cover with another towel, and pat the potatoes to dry them.

2. Pour the oil into the deep-fat fryer; the oil should be at least 2 inches (5 cm) deep. Heat the oil to 375°F (190°C). Slice by slice (so that the potatoes do not stick together in the oil), carefully drop a small handful of potato slices into the frying basket in the fryer. Fry the potatoes until crisp, about 2 minutes. Transfer the potatoes to several thicknesses of paper towel to drain. Immediately season the chips with sea salt, which will cling to the potatoes while they are still coated with a light film of fat. Repeat until all the potatoes have been fried, making sure that the oil temperature returns to 375°F (190°C) before continuing.

3. To serve, place a truffle slice on each of 20 potato chips. Serve the remaining potato chips as a snack.

    NOTE: *The amount of oil needed for deep-frying will depend on the size of the fryer. For these chips, I use a tiny fryer that holds only 1 quart (1 l) of oil.*

    WINE SUGGESTION: *Like almost anyone who loves wine and entertaining, I think a crystal flute filled with bubbling Champagne is always welcome. Serve the best you can afford. Your guests will applaud a Billecart-Salmon non-vintage rosé.*

"Truffles are to the soil as stars are to the sky."

—HENRI-FRÉDÉRIC BLANC, FRENCH AUTHOR, BORN MARSEILLE, 1954

SALADS

PINE NUT, PANCETTA, GOAT CHEESE,
AND TRUFFLE SALAD 42

BELGIAN ENDIVE, PINE NUT, CHIVE,
AND TRUFFLE SALAD 45

GREEN ZEBRA TOMATOES WITH PARMESAN AND
SUMMER TRUFFLES 48

WARM ARTICHOKE, PARMESAN, HAZELNUT OIL,
AND TRUFFLE SALAD 50

TRUFFLE, POTATO, AND WATERCRESS SALAD 53

PINE NUT, PANCETTA, GOAT CHEESE, AND TRUFFLE SALAD

This simple, elegant salad shows off all the best qualities of the truffle: its julienne slices glisten with a coating of fragrant pine nut oil, the larger pieces allow for that essential, pleasing crunch, and the color contrast with the golden pine nuts and soft green lettuce is oh so pleasing to the eye. The addition of warm, perfumed pancetta and firm, buttery goat's milk cheese all but gilds the lily.

4 SERVINGS

EQUIPMENT: *A small jar with a lid; a mandoline or a very sharp knife.*

1 fresh black truffle (about 1 ounce; 30 g), cleaned (see Note, page 26)

2/3 cup (100 g) pine nuts

About 3 tablespoons best-quality pine nut oil (preferably Leblanc brand)

Truffle Salt (page 186)

3/4 cup (2 1/2 ounces; 75 g) cubed pancetta

1 buttercrunch lettuce head, torn into pieces

4 ounces (120 g) firm goat's milk cheese, crumbled

3 tablespoons minced fresh chives

1. With a vegetable peeler, peel the truffle. Mince the truffle peelings, place them in the jar, and tighten the lid. Reserve the peelings for another use. With the mandoline or very sharp knife, cut the truffle into thick slices. Cut the slices into matchsticks.

2. Toast the pine nuts: Place the nuts in a small dry skillet and cook over medium heat, shaking the pan regularly, until they are fragrant and evenly toasted, about 2 minutes. Watch carefully! They can burn quickly.

3. Transfer the pine nuts to a bowl. Add the truffles. Toss with just enough pine nut oil to coat the ingredients lightly and evenly. Season lightly with the salt.

4. In a small dry skillet, brown the pancetta over medium heat until crisp and golden, about 5 minutes. With a slotted spoon, transfer the pancetta to several layers of paper towel. Blot the top of the pancetta to absorb any additional fat.

5. Place the lettuce in a large salad bowl. Add just enough pine nut oil to coat the greens lightly and evenly. Toss. Season lightly with the truffle salt. Arrange the dressed leaves on 4 individual salad plates. Shower with the pancetta, cheese, and chives. Top with the pine nut and truffle mixture. Serve.

"At the time I write, the glory of the truffle has now reached its culmination. Who would dare to say that he has been at a dinner where there was not a pièce truffée? Who has not felt his mouth water in hearing truffles à la Provençale spoken of? In the end, the truffle is the very diamond of gastronomy."

—JEAN-ANTHELME BRILLAT-SAVARIN, *THE PHYSIOLOGY OF TASTE* (1825)

BELGIAN ENDIVE, PINE NUT, CHIVE, AND TRUFFLE SALAD

This refreshing winter salad offers crunch, aroma, a fine blending of flavors, and a pleasing contrast of colors. Serve it as a first course, with plenty of crusty bread.

4 SERVINGS

EQUIPMENT: *A small jar with a lid; a mandoline or a very sharp knife.*

1 fresh black truffle (about 1 ounce; 30 g), cleaned (see Note, page 26)

1/3 cup (50 g) pine nuts

3 tablespoons minced fresh chives

Several tablespoons best-quality pine nut oil (preferably Leblanc brand)

Truffle Salt (page 186)

4 Belgian endive heads, trimmed

4 thin slices sourdough bread, toasted, for serving

1. With a vegetable peeler, peel the truffle. Mince the truffle peelings, place them in the jar, and tighten the lid. Reserve the peelings for another use. With the mandoline or very sharp knife, cut the truffle into thick slices. Cut the slices into matchsticks.

2. Toast the pine nuts: Place the nuts in a small dry skillet and cook over medium heat, shaking the pan regularly, until they are fragrant and evenly toasted, about 2 minutes. Watch carefully! They can burn quickly.

3. Transfer the pine nuts to a bowl. Add the truffles and chives. Toss with just enough pine nut oil to coat the ingredients lightly and evenly. Season lightly with the truffle salt.

4. Slice each endive head in half lengthwise. Place each half, cut side down, on the cutting board and cut on the diagonal into thick matchsticks. Place the endive in a large salad bowl. Add just enough pine nut oil to coat the greens lightly and evenly. Season lightly with the salt. Arrange the endive on 4 individual salad plates. Top with the pine nut, truffle, and chive mixture. Serve with the toast.

VARIATION: *For a colorful, heartier winter salad, add about 8 ounces (250 g) each of tiny haricots verts (green beans), blanched and refreshed; seared pancetta matchsticks; and seared fresh mushrooms.*

ON PRESERVING TRUFFLES

In the sixteenth century, truffles were enveloped in wax to prevent evaporation and also to preserve their aroma. But until the early nineteenth century, no one had been able to come up with a satisfactory method to preserve truffles. Drying or immersing in brine completely removed their flavor. Oil, lard, and sawdust also proved ineffective.

In 1810 Frenchman Nicolas Appert developed a preserving technique still in use today. Thick black glass bottles were created, with a narrow neck just wide enough to hold an average truffle. The jars were filled with whole truffles, sealed with a cork, and bound with a wire. The bottles were then stacked in a cauldron and covered with cold water that was gently brought to a boil, then cooled again. Once removed from the water, the bottles were sealed with red wax. Truffles could be kept for up to three years when preserved in this way.

"Cabassac grew inordinately happy whenever a light rain shower touched the parched earth towards the very end of spring. These rainfalls, he knew, would quench the thirst of the still minuscule tuber just long enough to bring the truffle to that critical moment in its development: that of the double Damos. The double Damos occurred between Nosto-Damo de L'Assoumcioun on August 15 and Nosto-Damo de la Navieta on September 8. During this period an abundant rain had to fall, for it is just then that truffle undergoes a period of exponential growth. With an overall rainfall, say, of five or six centimeters at this time, the truffle can grow between a hundred and a thousand times its size in just a matter of days. It is just at that moment that the truffle breaks free of its symbiotic relationship with its host, and becomes an autonomous growth unto itself."

—GUSTAF SOBIN, *THE FLY-TRUFFLER* (2001)

GREEN ZEBRA TOMATOES WITH PARMESAN AND SUMMER TRUFFLES

Raoul Reichrath, my favorite chef in our part of Provence, presented me with this simple, sublime truffle salad one warm summer evening in July. He layered thin slices of brilliant Green Zebra tomatoes and generously topped them with shards of aged Parmigiano-Reggiano cheese, wafers of fresh summer truffles, and a light shower of extra-virgin olive oil. A touch of minced chives and *fleur de sel*, and we were in heaven. The lime-emerald flesh of the heirloom Green Zebra and its sweet, almost spicy flavor created a perfect counterpoint to the earthy truffle and salty, lactic cheese.

4 SERVINGS

EQUIPMENT: *A small jar with a lid; a mandoline or a very sharp knife.*

1 or 2 fresh summer truffles (about 1 ounce; 30 g each), cleaned (see Note, page 26)

Extra-virgin olive oil

Truffle Salt (page 186)

8 Green Zebra tomatoes (about 1 1/2 pounds; 750 g total), cored and sliced crosswise

About 32 shavings of Parmigiano-Reggiano cheese

Grated zest of 1 lemon, preferably organic

3 tablespoons minced fresh chives

1. With a vegetable peeler, peel the truffle. Mince the truffle peelings, place them in the jar, and tighten the lid. Reserve the peelings for another use. With the mandoline or very sharp knife, cut the truffle into very thin slices.

2. Drizzle 4 salad plates with the oil and sprinkle with the truffle salt. Overlap the tomato slices on each plate. Season lightly with the salt and oil. Scatter with the cheese. Arrange the truffle slices on top. Season once more with oil and salt. Shower with the lemon zest and chives. Serve.

> **NON-TRUFFLE VARIATION:** *In place of truffles and truffle salt, use lemon salt, garnish with lemon zest, and top each salad with a few pitted black olives. Lovely color contrast, great forward flavors!*

"Whosoever says *truffle*, utters a grand word, which awakens erotic and gastronomic ideas."

—JEAN-ANTHELME BRILLAT-SAVARIN, *THE PHYSIOLOGY OF TASTE* (1825)

WARM ARTICHOKE, PARMESAN, HAZELNUT OIL, AND TRUFFLE SALAD

Artichokes are up there as one of my top ten foods. I eat them whenever I find them fresh in the market. The first-of-season baby artichokes usually appear at the end of February, just as fresh truffles are saying *au revoir* for the winter. That's when I prepare this luscious, full-flavored salad, a fine marriage of artichokes, cheese, fragrant hazelnut oil, and truffles.

4 SERVINGS

EQUIPMENT: *A small jar with a lid; a mandoline or a very sharp knife.*

1 fresh black truffle (about 1 ounce; 30 g), cleaned (see Note, page 26)

1 tablespoon freshly squeezed lemon juice

3 tablespoons extra-virgin olive oil

2 plump, fresh garlic cloves, peeled, halved, green germ removed, and minced

Fine sea salt

4 fresh globe artichokes, or 8 fresh baby artichokes

24 shavings of Parmigiano-Reggiano cheese

Truffle Salt (page 186)

1 tablespoon best-quality hazelnut oil (preferably Leblanc brand)

1. With a vegetable peeler, peel the truffle. Mince the truffle peelings, place them in the jar, and tighten the lid. Reserve the peelings for another use. With the mandoline or very sharp knife, cut the truffle into very thin slices.

2. In a bowl, combine the lemon juice, olive oil, garlic, and fine sea salt to taste.

3. Prepare the artichokes: As you would break off the tough ends of an asparagus spear, break off the stem of each artichoke to about 1 inch (2.5 cm) from the base. Carefully trim and discard the stem's fibrous exterior, leaving the edible and highly prized inner, almost-white stem. Cut off the top quarter of the artichoke. Bend back the tough outer green leaves, one at a time, letting them snap off naturally at the base. Continue snapping off leaves until only the central cone of yellow leaves with pale green tips remains. Lightly trim the top cone of leaves to just below the green tips. Trim any dark green areas from the base. Halve the artichoke lengthwise. With a grapefruit spoon or melon baller, scrape out, and discard, the hairy choke. Place the artichoke half, cut side down, on a clean work surface. With a very sharp knife, slice the halved artichoke lengthwise into paper-thin slices. Toss them in a bowl with the lemon, oil, and garlic mixture.

4. Heat a large dry skillet over medium heat. Add the artichokes and sauté until golden brown, 2 to 3 minutes.

5. Arrange 3 shavings of cheese on each of 4 salad plates. Arrange the artichokes on top of the cheese, top with the remaining cheese shavings, top with the truffle slices, season delicately with the truffle salt, and drizzle with the hazelnut oil. Serve as a first course or as a side vegetable dish.

TRUFFLE, POTATO, AND WATERCRESS SALAD

Potatoes and truffles are a classic combination: their life is in the soil, and earthiness is their best feature. This is a variation on the salad that Joël Robuchon made famous in the 1980s at his Paris restaurant Jamin. As ever, top-quality ingredients are essential.

4 SERVINGS

EQUIPMENT: *A mandoline or a very sharp knife; a small jar with a lid; a steamer.*

2 fresh black truffles (about 1 ounce; 30 g each), cleaned (see Note, page 26)

Truffle Salt (page 186)

3 tablespoons extra-virgin olive oil

1 tablespoon freshly squeezed lemon juice

About 10 ounces (300 g) yellow-fleshed potatoes (such as Yukon Gold)

3 cups (30 g) watercress leaves, rinsed and patted dry

1. With a vegetable peeler, peel the truffle. Mince the truffle peelings and place them in a large bowl. With the mandoline or very sharp knife, cut the truffle into very thin slices. Place the slices in the jar, and tighten the lid.

2. In a bowl, combine the minced truffle peelings, truffle salt to taste, the oil, and the lemon juice, and whisk to blend.

3. Scrub the potatoes but do not peel them. Bring 1 quart (1 l) of water to a simmer in the bottom of a steamer. Place the potatoes on the steaming rack. Place the rack over the simmering water, cover, and steam just until a skewer inserted into a potato comes away easily, 15 to 20 minutes.

4. While the potatoes are still hot, peel them and slice them into even 1-inch-thick (2.5 cm) rounds. Place them in the bowl with the truffle dressing, and toss thoroughly. Drain the potatoes, reserving the dressing. Dip the truffle slices into the reserved dressing.

5. In the center of each of 4 small salad plates, arrange the potato rounds side by side. On top of the potatoes, arrange several overlapping layers of truffles. Arrange the watercress in a ring around the potatoes and truffles. Season with the salt, and serve immediately.

"Plutarch, observing when and where the truffle was formed, agreed in principle that the truffle was formed by fusion, appearing at the exact point where a clap of thunder met a bolt of lightning."

—ELIZABETH LUARD, *TRUFFLES* (2006)

SOUPS

ARTICHOKE SOUP WITH PARMESAN AND TRUFFLES 58

PUMPKIN SOUP WITH TRUFFLE CREAM, CURRY,
PUMPKIN SEED OIL, AND TRUFFLES 61

PROVENÇAL WINTER PENICILLIN 63

SHELLFISH BROTH WITH TRUFFLES 65

SWEET ONION BROTH WITH SEARED FOIE GRAS
TOASTS AND TRUFFLES 67

VITO'S POTATO SOUP WITH PARMESAN CREAM
AND TRUFFLES 70

BRIN D'OLIVIER'S TRUFFLED CREAM SOUP 72

JERUSALEM ARTICHOKE SOUP WITH TRUFFLES 74

ARTICHOKE SOUP WITH PARMESAN AND TRUFFLES

Ever since I sampled this smooth, gorgeous soup at Guy Savoy's restaurant in Paris in the 1980s, it has been one of my perennial favorites. I prepare this year-round, sometimes even for myself for lunch, because it is so filling and fulfilling. I make it with fresh or frozen artichoke bottoms or even top-quality artichoke hearts from a jar or a can, which have the same rich flavor of fresh artichokes with none of the labor. Also, I *never* discard rinds of Parmesan: they add a delicious richness to the flavor of any soup.

12 SERVINGS

EQUIPMENT: *Cheesecloth; cotton twine; a small jar with a lid; a mandoline or a very sharp knife; a food mill fitted with a medium screen; 12 warmed shallow soup bowls.*

Several rinds of Parmigiano-Reggiano cheese

2 pounds (1 kg) artichoke hearts (about 12), fresh, from a jar or can, or frozen (no need to thaw)

2 quarts (2 l) Homemade Chicken Stock (page 195)

4 imported bay leaves

Fine sea salt

1 fresh black truffle (about 1 ounce; 30 g), cleaned (see Note, page 26)

One 2-ounce (60 g) chunk of Parmigiano-Reggiano cheese

1. Wrap the cheese rinds in the cheesecloth and secure with the cotton twine. In a large heavy-duty casserole, combine the cheesecloth bundle, artichokes (see page 51 for how to prepare fresh artichokes), stock, and bay leaves. Season lightly with sea salt.

Cover, and simmer just until the artichokes are soft and the flavors have had time to mingle, about 30 minutes. Taste for seasoning. Remove and discard the bay leaves and the cheesecloth bundle.

2. With a vegetable peeler, peel the truffle. Mince the truffle peelings, place them in the jar, and tighten the lid. Reserve the peelings for another use. With the mandoline or very sharp knife, cut the truffle into very thin slices.

3. Place the food mill over a large bowl and puree the soup into the bowl. (Discard any fibrous bits that remain in the mill.) Return the soup to the saucepan. The soup should be a pleasant golden green and should have the consistency of a thin puree. If too thin, reduce it slightly over moderate heat.

4. With a vegetable peeler, shave long, thick strips of the cheese onto a plate.

5. Ladle the soup into the bowls. Carefully place the cheese shavings on top of the soup. If done correctly, the shavings should sit delicately on top of the soup, half melted but still intact. Top with the truffle slices. Serve immediately.

"As a crop, the truffle marks the borderline where wilderness ends and cultivation begins. Neither truly wild nor truly cultivated, it can be encouraged but not coerced to fruit."

—ELIZABETH LUARD, *TRUFFLES* (2006)

PUMPKIN SOUP WITH TRUFFLE CREAM, CURRY, PUMPKIN SEED OIL, AND TRUFFLES

This seemingly simple soup turns exquisite, even elegant, with the added touch of curry powder, nutmeg, and cinnamon and a lovely cloud of truffle cream. Anoint the final serving with greenish-gold pumpkin seed oil and a final shower of truffles. I credit Joe Dolce, a student at one of our Truffle Weeks, for his creative embellishment.

8 SERVINGS

EQUIPMENT: *A food processor, a blender, or an immersion blender; a mandoline or a very sharp knife; 1 or 2 small jars with lids; a flat-mesh strainer; 8 warmed shallow soup bowls.*

2 pounds (1 kg) raw pumpkin, peeled and cubed (to yield 1 quart; 1 liter)

1 quart (1 l) Homemade Chicken Stock (page 195)

1 fresh black truffle (about 1 ounce; 30 g), cleaned (see Note, page 26)

1 cup (250 ml) Truffle Cream (page 189)

1 teaspoon Homemade Curry Powder (page 188)

1/4 teaspoon freshly ground nutmeg

2 teaspoons ground cinnamon

Fine sea salt

24 shavings of Parmigiano-Reggiano cheese

About 1 tablespoon best-quality pumpkin seed oil (preferably Leblanc brand)

1. In a stockpot, combine the pumpkin and the chicken stock, and bring to a boil over high heat. Cover, and boil until the pumpkin is soft, about 15 minutes.

2. Puree the mixture in a food processor, blender, or with an immersion blender until emulsified into a smooth-textured soup. (The soup may be prepared 1 day ahead of time up to this point. Store it in an airtight container in the refrigerator.)

3. With a vegetable peeler, peel the truffle. Mince the truffle peelings, place them in a jar, and tighten the lid. Reserve the peelings for another use. With the mandoline or very sharp knife, cut the truffle into thick slices. Cut the slices into matchsticks. If preparing the soup in advance, place the matchsticks in a jar and tighten the lid.

4. At serving time, return the mixture to the stockpot and bring to a boil again. With a flat-mesh strainer, skim off any scum that rises to the top. Add the truffle cream, curry powder, nutmeg, and cinnamon. Taste for seasoning, and add sea salt if needed. Place several shavings of Parmesan cheese in each of the soup bowls, and pour the soup over the cheese. Garnish with the truffle matchsticks and the pumpkin seed oil. Serve immediately.

Lord Byron (1788–1824) kept a truffle on his desk because he believed it fed his imagination.

PROVENÇAL WINTER PENICILLIN

There are winter days when it's colder in the south of France than in the north. On those days, we light a fire in the kitchen fireplace and I light the handy *coupe feu*, the center "simmer" burner on my La Cornue stove that allows me to simmer stocks and soups over very low heat. This is a favorite creation.

8 SERVINGS

EQUIPMENT: *Two small jars with lids; a mandoline or a very sharp knife; 8 warmed shallow soup bowls.*

2 fresh black truffles (about 1 ounce; 30 g each), cleaned (see Note, page 26)

2 quarts (2 l) Homemade Chicken Stock (page 195)

4 celery ribs, cut crosswise into very thin slices

6 Jerusalem artichokes (sunchokes), peeled and cut into even cubes

1 pound (500 g) domestic mushrooms, trimmed and cut into thin slices

Fine sea salt

12 ounces (375 g) dried egg noodles

Coarse, freshly ground black pepper

1/4 cup minced fresh flat-leaf parsley leaves

1. With a vegetable peeler, peel the truffles. Mince the truffle peelings, place them in a jar, and tighten the lid. With the mandoline or very sharp knife, cut the truffles into very thin slices. Place the slices in a jar, and tighten the lid.

2. In a stockpot, combine the stock, celery, Jerusalem artichokes, mushrooms, and 1 teaspoon of fine sea salt. Bring to a simmer, and simmer gently just until the

vegetables are soft, about 15 minutes. Add the noodles and simmer until cooked through, about 15 minutes more. Taste for seasoning, and add sea salt and pepper if needed.

3. Stir in the minced truffle peelings. Ladle the soup into 8 warmed demitasse cups or 4 soup bowls. Garnish each with minced parsley and truffle slices.

Gioacchino Rossini (1792–1868) called the truffle the Mozart of mushrooms. He is quoted as saying, "I have wept three times in my life. Once when my first opera failed. Once again, the first time I heard Paganini play the violin. And once when a truffled turkey fell overboard at a boating picnic."

SHELLFISH BROTH WITH TRUFFLES

This golden-orange shellfish broth forms the backbone of many truffle recipes, but it can also stand alone as a simple soup, topped with delicate disks of fresh truffles. It plays a starring role in my Truffle and Shellfish Cream (page 194).

2 QUARTS (2 L) BROTH

EQUIPMENT: *A wooden mallet; a small jar with a lid; a mandoline or a very sharp knife; a fine-mesh sieve; dampened cheesecloth.*

2 tablespoons extra-virgin olive oil

2 pounds (1 kg) lobster or shrimp shells, well rinsed

1 tablespoon fennel seeds

2 segments star anise

4 imported bay leaves

1 plump, moist garlic head, halved crosswise but not peeled

2 teaspoons fine sea salt

1 tablespoon Italian tomato paste

1 fresh black truffle (about 1 ounce; 30 g), cleaned (see Note, page 26)

1. In a large stockpot, heat the oil over moderate heat until hot but not smoking. Add the shells and sear until they turn a bright pink and are very fragrant, 2 to 3 minutes.

2. Add 4 quarts cold water and the fennel seeds, star anise, bay leaves, garlic, sea salt, and tomato paste. Bring to a boil and boil vigorously, uncovered, for 20 minutes. To extract maximum flavor from the shells, use the wooden mallet to crush and break up the shells. Taste occasionally for seasoning and strength.

3. With a vegetable peeler, peel the truffle. Mince the truffle peelings, place them in the jar, and tighten the lid. Reserve the peelings for another use. With the mandoline or very sharp knife, cut the truffle into thick slices. Cut the slices into matchsticks.

4. Line the fine-mesh sieve with dampened cheesecloth, and place the sieve over a large bowl. Ladle the broth and solids into the sieve, pressing down hard on the solids to extract the maximum juices and flavor. Discard the solids.

5. Taste for seasoning. Serve warm in small cups as an appetizer or in warmed shallow soup bowls as a first course. Garnish with the truffle matchsticks. (Store the broth, without the garnish, in an airtight container in the refrigerator for up to 1 day or in the freezer for up to 1 month.)

SWEET ONION BROTH WITH SEARED FOIE GRAS TOASTS AND TRUFFLES

The aromatic scent of sweet white onions and pungent celery leaves wafts through the winter kitchen as this simple, sublime soup bubbles away atop the stove. Here the onion is treated as the regal vegetable it is, not as a forgotten bystander. The celery adds a fine herbal flavor and aroma. This soup was inspired by a version I sampled one winter's evening at one of my favorite Paris bistros, L'Épigramme. That night we were served a delicate onion soup with a slab of seared foie gras. The marriage was heavenly.

6 SERVINGS

EQUIPMENT: *Two small jars with lids; a mandoline or a very sharp knife; a wire-mesh tea infuser; 6 warmed shallow soup bowls.*

1 fresh black truffle (1 ounce; 30 g), cleaned (see Note, page 26)

1 1/2 pounds (750 g) sweet white onions

3 tablespoons extra-virgin olive oil

2 teaspoons coarse sea salt

A handful of celery leaves

4 imported bay leaves

6 cups (1.5 l) Homemade Chicken Stock (page 195)

6 slices sourdough bread, cut into 3-inch (7.5 cm) rounds

About 1 teaspoon (5 g) Truffle Butter (page 191)

6 slices fresh duck foie gras, each 1/2 inch (1.25 cm) thick, cut into 3-inch (7.5 cm) rounds

1. With a vegetable peeler, peel the truffle. Mince the truffle peelings, place them in a jar, and tighten the lid. Reserve the peelings for another use. With the mandoline or very sharp knife, cut the truffle into thick slices. Cut the slices into matchsticks. Place the slices in a jar, and tighten the lid.

2. Peel the onions and halve them crosswise (at the equator). Place cut side down on a cutting board and cut into very thin slices.

3. In a stockpot, combine the onions, oil, and salt, and stir to coat the onions. Sweat—cook, covered, over low heat until soft and translucent—about 8 minutes, stirring occasionally so the onions do not scorch.

4. Encase the celery leaves and bay leaves in the wire-mesh tea infuser and add it to the stockpot. Add the stock, cover, and bring just to a boil. Reduce the heat to low. Simmer, covered, for 25 minutes. Taste for seasoning.

5. While the soup is cooking, toast the bread rounds. Spread the toasted rounds lightly with truffle butter, and top with the foie gras.

6. Remove the tea infuser. Pour the soup into the warmed soup bowls and sprinkle with the truffle matchsticks. Serve with the foie gras *tartines* alongside.

WINE SUGGESTION: *I will break the French rule of "no wine with soup." The foie gras just calls out for something as special as it is. My choice is a Meursault-Charmes from François Jobard, a festive and elegant wine that can stand up to the luxurious combination of foie gras and truffles.*

NAPOLÉON LEGEND

One day, a young lieutenant of Napoléon I revealed to the emperor that his father had nineteen children and that each child was born nine months after an evening of dining on truffled hen and drinking Champagne. Napoléon, having had difficulties in producing an heir, immediately called for a load of truffles to be brought from Sarlat and for the famous bird to be prepared. Nine months later his son, known as the King of Rome, was born (1811), and the young lieutenant was awarded the stripes of a colonel in a regiment of the Périgord.

VITO'S POTATO SOUP WITH PARMESAN CREAM AND TRUFFLES

Vito Mollica, the talented, inventive, and outgoing chef at the Four Seasons Hotel in Florence, served us this soup on the opening night of a special cooking class we held there with our good friend Rolando Beramendi. Like French chef Joël Robuchon, Vito favors the nutty flavor of the Ratte potato, a knobby, diminutive fingerling. Because they are tiny, peeling them demands a bit of time and patience, but the labor is well worth it. Vito served this soup with a golden crown of fragrant Parmesan cream and a dusting of minced truffles.

4 SERVINGS

EQUIPMENT: *A food processor, a blender, or an immersion blender; 4 warmed shallow soup bowls.*

4 tablespoons extra-virgin olive oil

6 large shallots (7 ounces; 200 g), peeled and thinly sliced

7 celery ribs (7 ounces; 200 g), diced

Fine sea salt

2 pounds (1 kg) small Ratte potatoes, peeled and diced (or use Yukon Gold)

2 imported bay leaves

1/2 cup (125 ml) crème fraîche or heavy cream

1/2 cup (50 g) freshly grated Parmigiano-Reggiano cheese

2 tablespoons (12 g) minced fresh black truffles or minced truffle peelings

Truffle Salt (page 186)

1. In a large saucepan, combine 3 tablespoons of the olive oil, the shallots, celery, and salt, and sweat—cook, covered, over low heat until the vegetables are soft and translucent—5 to 7 minutes. Add the potatoes to the saucepan. Add 1 quart (1 l) hot water to cover, along with the bay leaves. Simmer gently until the potatoes are soft, about 25 minutes, adding more water if necessary.

2. Pour the cream into a saucepan and bring it to a simmer over moderate heat. Whisk in the cheese, cooking for just 1 minute.

3. Remove and discard the bay leaves. Add the final tablespoon of oil to the potatoes. Puree the soup in a food processor, blender, or with an immersion blender.

4. Pour the potato soup into the bowls. Place a spoonful of the Parmesan cream in the center of each serving, and with the point of a small knife, create a swirl pattern in the soup. Garnish with the minced truffles and a light touch of truffle salt.

VARIATION: *Serve the soup as an appetizer in demitasse cups, topped with a touch of Parmesan cream and the minced truffles.*

"The truffle needs enormous care if it is to develop a tubercle. It needs just enough warmth, just enough cold spells, just enough rain, a few thunderstorms, a friendly tree, the right kind of soil, the right kind of ecosystem, gentle harvesting, and a skillful cook to bring out the best of the flavor."

—SABINE BUCQUET-GRENET AND FRANÇOISE DUBARRY,

THE LITTLE BOOK OF TRUFFLES (2001)

BRIN D'OLIVIER'S TRUFFLED CREAM SOUP

I first sampled a version of this ethereal concoction one wintry night at the cozy restaurant Le Brin d'Olivier, in our village of Vaison-la-Romaine in Provence. That evening the chef prepared this simple combination of chicken stock and cream, and topped it with a poached egg and truffles. Since then, I have used the soup as a poaching base for goat cheese–filled ravioli and for fresh briny oysters. Whatever you do, begin with a rich homemade chicken stock and fresh, thick crème fraîche. A few shards of freshly shaved Parmigiano-Reggiano and a gentle sprinkling of truffle salt add a final, festive flourish.

4 SERVINGS

EQUIPMENT: *4 warmed shallow soup bowls.*

1 quart (1 l) Homemade Chicken Stock (page 195)

1/4 cup (60 ml) crème fraîche or heavy cream

2 imported bay leaves

1/2 teaspoon fresh thyme leaves

8 large goat cheese–filled ravioli (optional variation)

8 large freshly shucked oysters (optional variation)

8 shavings Parmigiano-Reggiano cheese

1 tablespoon (6 g) minced fresh truffles

Truffle Salt (page 186)

4 poached eggs (page 85)

1. In a large saucepan, combine the stock, crème fraîche, bay leaves, and thyme leaves, and whisk to blend. Bring just to a simmer.

2. Remove and discard the bay leaves. Pour the soup into the warmed bowls. Garnish with the cheese, truffles, and a sprinkling of truffle salt.

3. Gently place a poached egg on top.

VARIATIONS: Place 8 large goat cheese–filled ravioli in the simmering soup, and poach gently until cooked to desired doneness. Remove and discard the bay leaves. Pour the soup and 2 ravioli into each warmed bowl and garnish with the cheese, truffles, and a sprinkling of truffle salt.

Place 8 large freshly shucked oysters in the simmering soup, and poach gently for just 30 seconds to 1 minute. Remove and discard the bay leaves. Pour the soup and 2 oysters into each warmed bowl and garnish with the cheese, truffles, and a sprinkling of truffle salt.

TRUFFLE MASS

Since 1946 the small Provençal village of Richerenches has been celebrating Saint Antoine's Day, in honor of the patron saint of truffles, on the first Sunday following January 15. Faithful followers congregate for mass as the church fills up with the scent of fresh truffles. Members of the congregation give whole truffles for the collection as the basket is passed around, the proceeds of which are donated to the parish for the upkeep of the church. After the service, the members of the Brotherhood of the Black Diamond and Gastronomy exit the church, dressed in full pageantry, and head to the town square to weigh and sell the truffles. In 2008, 4.5 kilos (10 pounds) of truffles were collected.

JERUSALEM ARTICHOKE SOUP WITH TRUFFLES

How can just three ingredients—one of them salt—taste so creamy, rich, and delicious? Years ago, when I was researching an article about vegetable recipes created by Michelin three-star chefs, Pierre Gagnaire demonstrated this simple, sublime, wintry Jerusalem artichoke soup. Over time, I have turned the thick soup into a sauce for pasta; reduced it a bit to serve as a fine vegetable puree; or thinned out the nutty liquid with stock, using it as a base for poaching fresh oysters or scallops. If truffles are not available, try a last-minute drizzle of fragrant hazelnut oil as a garnish.

Do the Jerusalem artichokes need to be peeled? The cook may choose. It is a tedious task to peel the gnarled, knobby vegetable, but it results in a pale golden soup. I rather like the little brown dots that float through the liquid if you do not peel them; they add a touch of character to the soup. Just be sure to scrub the vegetable well.

8 SERVINGS

EQUIPMENT: *A blender or a food processor; 8 warmed shallow soup bowls.*

2 quarts (2 l) whole milk

2 teaspoons fine sea salt

2 pounds (1 kg) Jerusalem artichokes (sunchokes), scrubbed and trimmed

2 tablespoons (12 g) minced fresh black truffles or minced truffle peelings, or 1 tablespoon best-quality hazelnut oil (preferably Leblanc brand)

1. Rinse a large saucepan with water, leaving a bit of water in the pan. (This will prevent the milk from scorching and sticking to the pan.) Pour the milk into the pan and add the sea salt.

2. Peel the Jerusalem artichokes, chop them coarsely, and immediately drop them into the milk. (This will stop the vegetable from turning brown as it is exposed to the air.) When all the Jerusalem artichokes are in the pan, place it over moderate heat and simmer gently until soft, 35 to 40 minutes. Watch carefully so the milk does not overflow the pan.

3. Transfer the mixture in small batches to the blender or food processor. Do not place the plunger in the feed tube of the food processor, or the insert in the top of the blender, or the heat will create a vacuum and the liquid will splatter. Puree until the mixture is perfectly smooth and silky, 1 to 2 minutes.

4. Return the soup to the saucepan and reheat it gently. Taste for seasoning. Pour it into the warmed soup bowls and shower with the minced truffle or drizzle with the hazelnut oil.

VARIATIONS—A SOUP, A SAUCE, A VEGETABLE SIDE DISH: *This soup can easily be transformed into a sauce for pasta or into a puree to serve as a vegetable side dish. Simply reduce the soup over low heat to the desired thickness, 5 to 10 minutes.*

EGGS AND CHEESE

SCRAMBLED EGGS WITH TRUFFLES 78

FRESH GOAT CHEESE AND TRUFFLE OMELET 82

CREAMY POLENTA WITH TRUFFLES AND POACHED EGGS 85

PARMESAN, PINE NUT, AND TRUFFLE GRATINS 87

BAKED EGGS WITH PINE NUTS, SPROUTS, AND TRUFFLES 91

MOLLYCODDLED EGGS WITH TRUFFLES 95

RICOTTA *GNUDI* WITH HERBS AND TRUFFLES 99

TRUFFLED SAINT-MARCELLIN 101

TRUFFLED CHAOURCE 105

TRUFFLED VACHERIN DU MONT D'OR 107

TÊTE DE MOINE WITH CURRIED WALNUTS AND TRUFFLES 109

SCRAMBLED EGGS WITH TRUFFLES

Scrambled eggs are certainly one of the ten best ways to enjoy and appreciate truffles. The creamy richness of farm-fresh eggs, the seduction of the truffle butter, and the crunch of the fresh truffle all unite to create a powerful, satisfying dish, one good enough to worship.

2 SERVINGS

EQUIPMENT: *Two small jars with lids; a mandoline or a very sharp knife; 2 warmed salad plates.*

1 fresh black truffle (about 1 ounce; 30 g), cleaned (see Note, page 26)

6 large ultra-fresh eggs, preferably organic and free range, at room temperature (see Note)

2 tablespoons (1 ounce, 30 g) Truffle Butter (page 191), cut into small pieces

Truffle Salt (page 186)

2 slices Brioche (page 178), toasted and spread with Truffle Butter, for serving

1. With a vegetable peeler, peel the truffle. Mince the truffle peelings, place them in a jar, and tighten the lid. With the mandoline or very sharp knife, cut the truffle into thick slices. Cut the slices into matchsticks. Place the matchsticks in a jar, and tighten the lid.

2. Crack the eggs into a bowl, leaving the yolks whole. Add the truffle butter, the minced truffle peelings, and about 1/2 teaspoon truffle salt. Do not whisk or blend the mixture.

3. Pour the mixture into a large unheated nonstick skillet. Place the skillet over medium heat and stir gently but constantly with a wooden spoon until the eggs form a creamy

mass. Do not overcook. The entire process should take about 4 minutes. Stir in the truffle matchsticks. Taste for seasoning. With a large spoon, transfer the mixture to the warmed salad plates. Serve with the toasted brioche.

NOTE: *To infuse the eggs with truffle aroma and flavor, store a whole fresh truffle and the eggs (in their shells) in an airtight container in the refrigerator for at least 2 days and up to 1 week.*

WINE SUGGESTION: *Champagne is in order here, the best bottle you can afford. A house favorite is Bruno Paillard's rosé première cuvée, with a long finish that holds up to this sublime dish.*

PROVERB

Quand il pleut le jour de la Saint Roch (16 août), les truffes naissent sur le roc.

When it rains on the day of Saint Roch (August 16), truffles are born beneath the rocks.

—JEAN PAGNOL, *LA TRUFFE* (1983)

"When you feel like eating
boiled eggs, if you have
some truffles in the house,
put them in a basket with
the eggs and the next
day you will have the best
boiled eggs you have ever
tasted in your gastronomic
life."

—M. DES OMBIAUX,
BELGIAN FOOD AND WINE
WRITER (1868–1943)

FRESH GOAT CHEESE AND TRUFFLE OMELET

This is a favorite lunchtime treat for Walter and me, using a small amount of whichever truffle is in season. It's a nice way to get a serious hit of truffle flavor and texture—with the mushroom cut into thick matchsticks—using just a bit of truffle. A light seasoning of truffle salt helps extend the flavor.

2 SERVINGS

EQUIPMENT: *A 10-inch (25.5 cm) nonstick omelet or crepe pan; a large warmed plate.*

2 ounces (60 g) fresh goat's milk cheese

1 large ultra-fresh egg yolk, preferably organic and free range, at room temperature (see Note)

3/4 ounce (20 g) fresh black truffle matchsticks

Truffle Salt (page 186) or fine sea salt

3 large ultra-fresh eggs (see Note), at room temperature

2 teaspoons extra-virgin olive oil

1. On a small plate, mash the cheese and the egg yolk with a fork. Add the truffle matchsticks and ¼ teaspoon truffle salt. Mash again to blend the ingredients.

2. Crack the whole eggs into a bowl. Beat the eggs lightly with a fork (not a whisk), just enough to combine the yolks and whites well without incorporating air bubbles that might make the omelet dry out.

3. In the omelet pan, heat the oil over medium heat until warm. Add the eggs, tilting the pan from side to side to evenly coat the bottom. Cook just until the eggs are evenly

set but still slightly liquid on top, about 1 minute. Remove the pan from the heat. Quickly spoon the cheese, salt, and truffle mixture in a strip down the center of the omelet, in line with the pan's handle. With a fork, carefully fold the omelet over the filling from each side. Tip the pan up against the edge of the warmed plate so that the omelet rolls out browned side up. Season with truffle salt. Cut in half and serve immediately.

NOTE: *To infuse the eggs with truffle aroma and flavor, store a whole fresh truffle and the eggs (in their shells) in an airtight container in the refrigerator for at least 2 days and up to 1 week.*

WINE SUGGESTION: *Although this is not an "everyday" sort of dish, it goes fine with any everyday white, such as the fine* vin de pays *from Denis Alary in Cairanne. His cuvée Font d'Estévenas is made up of 65 percent Roussanne, filled out with Viognier and Clairette. It's a zesty lunch wine with a good balance of fruit and acidity.*

RAIN AND TRUFFLES

An ancient dictum says that for truffles to flourish, rain must touch the soil once between June 25 and 30, and again between July 14 and 20. And a good rain in August ensures an abundant crop.

"The *Tuber melanosporum* is an exception, a whim of nature, a black mushroom without stem or roots that develops mysteriously underground. Its firm flesh bears the smoothness and complexity of a silken weave and its unusual aroma is wild and entrancing."

—ALAIN DUCASSE, FRENCH CHEF

CREAMY POLENTA WITH TRUFFLES
AND POACHED EGGS

A creamy dish of warming, fragrant polenta is a standby in our home in the winter months. Sometimes we top it with a fiery tomato sauce or, as here, embellish it with fresh black truffles and a truffle-infused poached egg.

4 SERVINGS

EQUIPMENT: *Two small jars with lids; a mandoline or a very sharp knife; 4 warmed shallow soup bowls; four 1/4-cup (60 ml) ramekins.*

1 fresh black truffle (about 1 ounce; 30 g), cleaned (see Note, page 26)

2 cups (500 ml) whole milk

2 cups (500 ml) light cream

1 1/2 teaspoons fine sea salt

1/2 teaspoon freshly grated nutmeg

3/4 cup (135 g) quick-cooking Italian polenta

1 cup (100 g) freshly grated Parmigiano-Reggiano cheese

1 tablespoon distilled white vinegar

4 large ultra-fresh eggs, preferably organic and free range, at room temperature (see Note)

Truffle Salt (page 186)

1. Preheat the oven to 250°F (120°C).

2. With a vegetable peeler, peel the truffle. Mince the truffle peelings, place them in a jar, and tighten the lid. With the mandoline or very sharp knife, cut the truffle into very thin slices. Place the slices in a jar, and tighten the lid.

3. In a large saucepan, bring the milk, cream, 1 teaspoon of the sea salt, and the nutmeg to a simmer over medium heat. (Watch carefully, for milk will boil over quickly.) Add the polenta in a steady stream and, stirring constantly with a wooden spoon, cook until the mixture begins to thicken, about 3 minutes.

4. Remove from the heat. Add the cheese and the minced truffle peelings, stirring to blend thoroughly. The polenta should be very creamy and pourable. Spoon it into the warmed soup bowls. Place the bowls in the oven to keep warm.

5. In a large deep skillet, bring 2 inches (5 cm) of water to a boil. Reduce the heat to maintain a simmer, and add the vinegar and the remaining 1/2 teaspoon sea salt. Break the eggs into the ramekins, and one by one, carefully lower the lip of each ramekin into the water, letting the egg flow out. Turn off the heat and cover the pan. Poach the eggs until the whites are firm but the yolks are still runny and are covered with a thin translucent layer of white, about 3 minutes for medium-firm yolks and 5 minutes for firm yolks. With a slotted spoon, carefully lift the eggs from the water, drain, and place on each serving of polenta. Shower with the truffle slices and season with truffle salt. Serve immediately.

NOTE: *To infuse the eggs with truffle aroma and flavor, store a whole fresh truffle and the eggs (in their shells) in an airtight container in the refrigerator for at least 2 days and up to 1 week.*

VARIATION: *Morel mushrooms cooked in cream are delicious in place of the truffles.*

WINE SUGGESTION: *Once while preparing this dish I was sipping the day's aperitif white, the Perrin brothers' Réserve Blanc, an elegant, complex white Côtes du Rhône, a brilliant blend of Grenache Blanc, Bourboulenc, Marsanne, Roussanne, and Viognier.*

PARMESAN, PINE NUT, AND TRUFFLE GRATINS

I generally recommend that truffle slices not be cooked, for they will lose two of their greatest attributes: crunch and aroma. But here the truffles are first moistened in pine nut oil (a nutty flavor that marries beautifully with the mushroom) and then hidden between layers of moist Parmesan cheese, which serves as a protective barrier as the tiny gratins are heated just until the cheese melts. Serve these gratins as an opening act, as a first course with a salad, or, as here, as the cheese course with a tangy watercress salad alongside.

4 SERVINGS

EQUIPMENT: *Two small jars with lids; a mandoline or a very sharp knife; four 1/4-cup (60 ml) ramekins; a baking sheet.*

1 fresh black truffle (about 1 ounce; 30 g), cleaned (see Note, page 26)

Several tablespoons best-quality pine nut oil (preferably Leblanc brand)

1/3 cup (50 g) pine nuts

3 cups (30 g) watercress leaves, rinsed and patted dry

Truffle Salt (page 186)

1/2 cup (50 g) freshly grated Parmigiano-Reggiano cheese

1. With a vegetable peeler, peel the truffle. Mince the truffle peelings, place them in a jar, and tighten the lid. Reserve the peelings for another use. With the mandoline or very sharp knife, cut the truffle into very thin slices. Place the slices in a jar, and cover with 1 tablespoon (15 ml) of the oil. Tighten the lid, and shake the jar to coat

the truffle slices. Marinate at room temperature for 5 to 10 minutes. The oil will moisten the truffles and prevent them from drying out while the gratin is cooking.

2. Arrange a rack in the oven about 3 inches (7.5 cm) from the heat source. Preheat the broiler.

3. Toast the pine nuts: Place the nuts in a small dry skillet over medium heat and cook, shaking the pan regularly, until they are fragrant and evenly toasted, about 2 minutes. Watch carefully! They can burn quickly. Transfer the nuts to a small plate to cool.

4. Place the watercress in a salad bowl and toss with just enough pine nut oil to coat the leaves lightly and evenly. Season delicately with truffle salt.

5. Place the ramekins side by side on the baking sheet. Using half of the cheese, drop a sprinkling of cheese into each of the ramekins. Sprinkle with the pine nuts. Top with the truffle slices and their oil. Sprinkle with the remaining cheese.

6. Place the baking sheet under the broiler and broil just until the cheese is golden and bubbly, about 1 minute. Transfer the ramekins to a dinner plate. Serve immediately, with the watercress salad alongside.

WINE SUGGESTION: *Our winemaker, Yves Gras, makes a welcome Sablet Blanc, a chalky wine that loves truffles. A blend of Viognier, Bourboulenc, Grenache Blanc, and Clairette, much of it is grown in the sandy soils of Sablet (thus the town's name, Sable, is French for "sand"). It is a pleasing wine that seems to go with everything.*

TRUFFLES AND POACHERS

The absence of fences in Provence creates a problem: how to protect *truffières* from poachers? This problem is, however, regulated by law. Since the late 1980s the tribunal of Aix-en-Provence has imposed heavy prison sentences and fines of up to 1,000 euros for truffle theft. Theft being more difficult in cultivated truffle farms, poachers have to employ many tricks. Stealing truffles *à la cape* illustrates this well: Poachers will enter a truffle farm late at night wearing a cape or large cloak. Kneeling or crouching at the roots of the trees, they pull the edges of the cloak over the area where they will dig, taking care to make sure the two sides of the cloak meet. Now protected from view, they can dig, with a flashlight in hand, undisturbed. Many poachers, rather than putting the stolen truffles in their pockets or bags, find a place near the truffle farm where they can bury the truffles, storing them safely until market day.

BAKED EGGS WITH PINE NUTS, SPROUTS, AND TRUFFLES

One cold day in January, Walter and I ran into our friend Juan Sanchez on the streets of Paris, and we decided to grab a quick lunch together at Le Comptoir, a popular neighborhood bistro. That day, a version of these baked eggs with truffles was on the menu. We ordered them, fell in love, and now the dish appears on our family table with great frequency. Eggs and pine nuts have long been favored escorts for truffles, but it never would have occurred to me to add the sprouts as a fresh "frill." As it happens, they round out the dish, offering a fine touch of texture and flavor.

4 SERVINGS

EQUIPMENT: *Two small jars with lids; a mandoline or a very sharp knife; four 6-inch (15-cm) round baking dishes; a baking sheet.*

1 fresh black truffle (about 1 ounce; 30 g), cleaned (see Note, page 26)

2 tablespoons (30 g) Truffle Butter (page 191), at room temperature

8 large ultra-fresh eggs, preferably organic and free range, at room temperature (see Note)

1/3 cup (50 g) pine nuts

Several tablespoons fresh lentil sprouts or microgreens, rinsed and patted dry

1 tablespoon minced green scallion tops or minced fresh chives

Truffle Salt (page 186)

8 Thin Bread Crisps (page 182), for serving

1. Center a rack in the oven. Preheat the oven to 325°F (165°C).

2. With a vegetable peeler, peel the truffle. Mince the truffle peelings, place them in a jar, and tighten the lid. Reserve the peelings for another use. With the mandoline or very sharp knife, cut the truffle into very thin slices. Place the slices in a jar, and tighten the lid.

3. Butter the baking dishes with the truffle butter. Crack 2 eggs into each dish, taking care not to break the yolks. Arrange the baking dishes side by side on the baking sheet, and place it in the oven. Bake until the whites are firm around the edges and the yolks are just slightly set but still runny, 8 to 10 minutes.

4. While the eggs are baking, toast the pine nuts: Place the nuts in a small dry skillet and cook over medium heat, shaking the pan regularly, until they are fragrant and evenly toasted, about 2 minutes. Watch carefully! They can burn quickly.

5. Remove the baking sheet from the oven. Shower the eggs with the pine nuts, sprouts, and scallions. Evenly divide the sliced truffles among the dishes, and season lightly with truffle salt. Serve with the bread crisps.

NOTE: *To infuse the eggs with truffle aroma and flavor, store a whole fresh truffle and the eggs (in their shells) in an airtight container in the refrigerator for at least 2 days and up to 2 weeks.*

WINE SUGGESTION: *I don't remember which wine Juan chose that day, but it might well have been a mineral-rich Chablis, a wine that pairs well with the earthy flavor of the truffle. Favorites come from the vineyards of Jean-Claude Bessin, René and Vincent Dauvissat, and François Raveneau.*

"Now Roseline was the only sow in the district that was likely to die of old age. Her huge thighs would never be rubbed with salt to be cured with saltpeter and turned into hams. Her fat would never be melted down into lard. Roseline was one of those rarest of females that dug up truffles without eating them, except of course when she was given one as a reward. Even then you had to be prudent for fear of destroying her sense of smell, for just as the drunkard will never be able to tell a Château Latour from a Château Haut-Brion, Roseline would soon lose the ability to detect truffles in the soil if she were given too many."

—PIERRE MAGNAN, *DEATH IN THE TRUFFLE WOOD* (2006)

MOLLYCODDLED EGGS WITH TRUFFLES

Wow, recipes don't get simpler than this, or more flavorful! Once I discovered this simple steamed egg concept, it has become a staple in our house—breakfast, lunch, or dinner. The possibilities are endless. Truffles are of course a luxury, but equally wonderful are toppings of spinach, mushrooms, garden herbs, or bits of cooked pancetta or bacon.

8 SERVINGS

EQUIPMENT: *A small jar with a lid; a mandoline or a very sharp knife; eight 1/2-cup (125 ml) ovenproof ramekins, egg coddlers, custard cups, tea cups, or* petits pots; *a steamer.*

1 fresh black truffle (about 1 ounce; 30 g), cleaned (see Note, page 26)

2 tablespoons (30 g) Truffle Butter (page 191), at room temperature

8 large ultra-fresh eggs, preferably organic and free range, at room temperature (see Note)

8 thin slices of Brioche (page 178)

Truffle Salt (page 186)

1. With a vegetable peeler, peel the truffle. Mince the truffle peelings, place them in the jar, and tighten the lid. Reserve the peelings for another use. With the mandoline or very sharp knife, cut the truffle into very thin slices. The truffle should yield about 20 slices.

2. Lightly butter with truffle butter the insides of the ramekins. Break an egg into each ramekin, taking care not to break the yolks. Place the truffle slices on top of the eggs.

3. Bring 1 quart (1 l) of water to a simmer in the bottom of a steamer. Place the steaming rack over the simmering water. Arrange the ramekins—uncovered—side by side on the steaming rack. Cover the steamer, and cook the eggs just until partially

set—with the whites firm around the edges and the yolks covered with a thin film of white—10 to 12 minutes.

4.   While the eggs are steaming, toast the brioche and butter the slices lightly with truffle butter.

5.   Transfer the ramekins to a small plate, season each one lightly with truffle salt, and serve immediately, with the buttered brioche alongside.

NOTE: *To infuse the eggs with truffle aroma and flavor, store a whole fresh truffle and the eggs (in their shells) in an airtight container in the refrigerator for at least 2 days and up to 1 week.*

WINE SUGGESTION: *When we made these during my latest truffle class, we paired them with the honey-scented white Châteauneuf-du-Pape Domaine Grand Veneur, a special cuvée made with 100 percent Roussanne.*

"Now approaching the very end of the season, beating the grasses for the furtive trace of some evanescent mousco, Cabassac came upon the last black truffle of the year. He'd waited until a fly (heavy with eggs undoubtedly) had returned to its perched station three successive times, then—at that very spot—had dug a full forty centimeters straight down. The earth itself grew more and more pungent as he went. Too pungent, he thought to himself. And, sure enough, when he finally unearthed this last tuber of the year, its ripeness—he immediately detected—bordered on putrescence. It was several days past maturity. Held up to his nostrils, its scent, indeed, was overwhelming. Far more animal than vegetable, it smelt—in turn—of musk, sperm, fuming meats."

—GUSTAF SOBIN, *THE FLY-TRUFFLER* (2001)

RICOTTA *GNUDI* WITH HERBS AND TRUFFLES

When Walter and I offered a special cooking week at the Four Seasons Hotel in Florence, chef Vito Mollica taught us these wonderful little ricotta *gnudi*, tiny balls of heaven that are basically ravioli filling without the pasta. They come together in a matter of minutes, and are about as versatile as a dish can get. The *gnudi* can be poached lightly in homemade chicken stock as I do here, then served with plenty of sliced truffles and shavings of Parmigiano-Reggiano cheese. Or, simply simmer them in a sublime tomato sauce. The recipe can easily be doubled for a crowd. And they freeze beautifully: Ever since I began making these at home, I have kept a batch of them in the freezer for a quick, no-nonsense dinner.

4 SERVINGS

EQUIPMENT: *A small jar with a lid; a mandoline or a very sharp knife; 4 warmed shallow soup bowls.*

1 pound (500 g) fresh sheep's milk ricotta

2/3 cup (95 g) unbleached all-purpose flour

1/2 cup (50 g) freshly grated Parmigiano-Reggiano cheese

1 large ultra-fresh egg yolk, preferably organic and free range, at room temperature (see Note)

1/2 teaspoon fine sea salt

1/4 cup minced mixed fresh herbs, such as chives, mint, and flat-leaf parsley

1/8 teaspoon freshly ground nutmeg

1 fresh black truffle (about 1 ounce; 30 g), cleaned (see Note, page 26)

2 quarts (2 l) Homemade Chicken Stock (page 195)

About 24 shavings of Parmigiano-Reggiano cheese

Truffle Salt (page 186)

1. On a large plate, combine the ricotta, flour, grated cheese, egg yolk, sea salt, herbs, and nutmeg. Mash with a fork to blend. With the palms of your hands, roll the mixture into balls about the size of a golf ball, about 2 ounces (60 g) each. You should have about 20 *gnudi*. (The *gnudi* can be made in advance and stored in an airtight container in the refrigerator for up to 1 day or in the freezer for up to 2 weeks. After that time they will lose their luster.)

2. At serving time, prepare the truffle: With a vegetable peeler, peel the truffle. Mince the truffle peelings, place them in the jar, and tighten the lid. Reserve the peelings for another use. With the mandoline or very sharp knife, slice the truffle into very thin rounds.

3. In a shallow saucepan that is large enough to hold all the *gnudi*, bring the stock to a simmer over medium heat. Drop the fresh or frozen *gnudi* into the stock and simmer gently, 3 to 4 minutes for fresh *gnudi*, about 6 minutes for frozen *gnudi*. To serve, ladle the stock into the bowls. Place 4 or 5 *gnudi* in each bowl. Shower with the cheese shavings, truffle slices, and a delicate sprinkling of truffle salt.

NOTE: *To infuse the egg yolk with truffle aroma and flavor, store a whole fresh truffle and an egg (in its shell) in an airtight container in the refrigerator for at least 2 days and up to 1 week.*

WINE SUGGESTION: *On that same trip to Florence we were fortunate enough to visit the historic Villa di Capezzana on their first day of olive oil pressing. Of course we had to sample wine as well, and their red Carmignano—80 percent Sangiovese and 20 percent Cabernet Sauvignon—full of ripe cherry flavors, is a full-bodied wine that's ample enough to pair with these favored gnudi.*

TRUFFLED SAINT-MARCELLIN

Ever since I began working with truffles in the early 1980s, this has been an annual standby. Saint-Marcellin is a deliciously creamy disk of raw cow's milk cheese made in small dairies in France's Dauphiné, and its faintly lactic flavor and softness pair perfectly with the crunch of the truffle. Be sure to chill the cheese well, to ensure even slicing. Other cheeses that can be prepared in the same way include Rocamadour, a goat's milk cheese from the southwest of France; fresh Chavignol, a goat's milk cheese from the Loire Valley; and fresh Pélardon, a goat's milk cheese from Provence.

4 SERVINGS

EQUIPMENT: *A small jar with a lid; a mandoline or a very sharp knife; unflavored dental floss or a very sharp knife; a baking sheet.*

1 fresh black truffle (about 1 ounce; 30 g), cleaned (see Note, page 26)

4 disks Saint-Marcellin cow's milk cheese, well chilled

4 slices Brioche (page 178), toasted, for serving

1. With a vegetable peeler, peel the truffle. Mince the truffle peelings, place them in the jar, and tighten the lid. Reserve the peelings for another use. With the mandoline or very sharp knife, cut the truffle into very thin slices. The truffle should yield about 20 slices.

2. With the dental floss or very sharp knife, carefully slice one of the cheeses in half at the equator, like a layer cake. Arrange about 5 truffle slices over the bottom half of the cheese. Replace the top half of the cheese. Wrap it securely in plastic wrap. Repeat for the remaining cheeses. Refrigerate for 24 to 48 hours to perfume the cheese with the truffles.

3. At serving time, arrange a rack in the oven about 3 inches (7.5 cm) from the heat source. Preheat the broiler.

4. Unwrap the cheeses and transfer them to the baking sheet. Place the baking sheet under the broiler. As soon as the cheese begins to melt—about 1 minute—remove from the oven. With a spatula, carefully transfer the cheeses to small individual salad plates. Serve immediately, with the toasted brioche.

WINE SUGGESTION: *A young red Rhône wine is ideal here. A current favorite comes from our own winemaker, Yves Gras, whose light, fruit-forward Côtes du Rhône Les Quatre Terres—from four parcels in various villages, including Vacqueyras, Séguret, Roaix, and Rasteau—is primarily a blend of Grenache and Syrah.*

"Since, during storms, flames leap from the humid vapors and dark clouds emit deafening noises, is it surprising that the lightning, when it strikes the ground, gives rise to truffles, which do not resemble plants?"

—PLUTARCH, GREEK HISTORIAN (AD 46–120)

TRUFFLED CHAOURCE

Cheese and truffles are ideal mates because cheese virtually inhales the intense truffle aroma and the fat in the cheese fixes the flavor of the mushroom. Chaource is a double-cream cow's milk cheese, with just a touch more butterfat—50 percent as opposed to 45 percent for most cheeses. It is a beautiful white cylinder with a soft rind and a creamy, delicate interior. It has an exhilarating aroma of mushrooms and fresh walnuts. During truffle season, we serve this at most dinner parties—and of course during our truffle class in January—always to raves.

24 SERVINGS

EQUIPMENT: *A small jar with a lid; a mandoline or a very sharp knife; unflavored dental floss or a very sharp knife.*

2 fresh black truffles (about 1 ounce; 30 g each), cleaned (see Note, page 26)

1 Chaource cheese (1 pound; 500 g), well chilled

1. With a vegetable peeler, peel the truffles. Mince the truffle peelings, place them in the jar, and tighten the lid. Reserve the peelings for a final garnish on the cheese. With the mandoline or very sharp knife, cut the truffles into very thin slices. Each truffle should yield about 20 slices.

2. With the dental floss or very sharp knife, carefully cut the cheese crosswise into 3 even disks, like a layer cake. Layer the truffle slices on each of the 2 lower slices of cheese, reconstructing the cheese by adding the top slice. Wrap it securely in plastic wrap. Refrigerate for 24 to 48 hours to perfume the cheese with the truffles.

3. To serve, remove the cheese from the refrigerator and let it come to room temperature. Unwrap and place on a cheese tray. Sprinkle with the minced truffle peelings. Serve, cutting into thin wedges.

WINE SUGGESTION: *A red Burgundy is often advised with the chubby Chaource cheese. A favorite comes from winemaker Ghislaine Barthod; her no-nonsense Bourgogne displays the flavors of raspberries and cherries, a pure wine with a hint of smokiness, a nice touch with the truffles.*

"Presently, we were aware of an odour gradually coming towards us, something musky, fiery, savoury, mysterious—a hot drowsy smell, that lulls the senses, and yet enflames them—the truffles were coming."

—WILLIAM MAKEPEACE THACKERAY, BRITISH NOVELIST (1811–1863),

IN *MEMORIALS OF GOURMANDISING*

TRUFFLED VACHERIN DU MONT D'OR

When French food lovers return from their summer vacations at the end of August, they are already looking forward to the first-of-season Mont d'Or, a cow's milk cheese that appears in the best cheese shops in mid-September, reigning until the middle of May. This creamy, smooth cheese, held in place with a thin spruce band and placed in a wooden box, is known officially as Vacherin du Mont d'Or and is made on the French side of the border between France and Switzerland. Its richness, the slight hint of pine, and its seasonality make it an ideal match for winter truffles. Vacherin comes in three sizes, weighing from 12 ounces (375 g) to 6.6 pounds (3 kg). The smaller cheeses are purchased whole, while the large cheeses are sold by the wedge in cheese shops.

12 SERVINGS

1 small (12-ounce; 375 g) Vacherin du Mont d'Or cheese

1 teaspoon mascarpone cheese

2 teaspoons minced fresh black truffles or minced truffle peelings

Fine sea salt

16 thin fresh black truffle slices

1. With a knife, remove and discard the crust from the cheese. Scoop about one fourth of the cheese out from the center and place it in a bowl.

2. Add the mascarpone and minced truffles to the bowl, and mash with a fork. Taste for seasoning, adding a pinch of salt if necessary. Spoon the mixture back into the cheese. Cover securely with plastic wrap and refrigerate for at least 6 hours or up to 2 days.

3. Remove the cheese from the refrigerator 2 hours before serving. Arrange the truffle slices on top of the cheese. Serve, letting guests spoon individual servings straight from the box.

WINE SUGGESTION: *A fruity white wine from the Savoie region of France would be the perfect match: look for Raymond Quénard's Chignin-Bergeron, a 100 percent Roussanne wine that's creamy and luscious and right at home with the truffles and cheese.*

"Plant acorns, and you will have truffles."

—ADRIEN DE GASPARIN, FRENCH AGRONOMIST

AND POLITICIAN (1783–1862)

TÊTE DE MOINE WITH CURRIED WALNUTS AND TRUFFLES

Sometimes recipes are born in the most amazing ways. Around 5 o'clock each afternoon as I sit working at my computer, my tummy rumbles to suggest it might need some sustenance. Frequently "on the menu" will be a tiny bowl of my current favorite: curried pumpkin seeds, made with my homemade curry powder. One day that tiny bowl did not suffice, so I headed back to the refrigerator and found a golden round of Tête de Moine cheese begging to be sliced. I turned it into little curls and placed them in the bowl that once held the pumpkin seeds. A touch of curry powder remained at the bottom of the bowl, and when I sampled the cheese, my palate experienced an explosion of flavors as the fattiness of the cheese and the exotic notes of curry created an entire symphony of sensations. Soon after, I perfected this combination of curried walnuts paired with thin curls of cheese and a slice of truffle. The combination can be served as a cheese course, with several curls of cheese topped with walnuts and truffles, or as an appetizer, with a curl of cheese, a walnut, and a truffle slice speared with a toothpick.

6 SERVINGS

32 thin ruffles of Tête de Moine cheese, cut with a cheese *girolle* (see Note) or a very sharp knife

1 cup (125 g) Curried Walnuts (recipe follows)

About 16 fresh black truffle slices

For a cheese course, arrange the cheese ruffles on salad plates. Scatter with the walnut halves, then the truffle slices.

For an appetizer, spear a walnut, several cheese ruffles, and a truffle slice with a toothpick.

NOTE: *A cheese* girolle *can be purchased from my Amazon Store via www.patriciawells.com.*

WINE SUGGESTION: *The intensely flavored Tête de Moine favors a big red, such as a Châteauneuf-du-Pâpe. Two favorites come from the vineyards of Domaine de la Janasse and Domaine de la Mordorée.*

CURRIED WALNUTS

When cooking, I follow the adage that "what grows together goes together." Walnuts and truffles thrive in the same soil and climate, so their marriage is a natural. These curried treats find their way into many of my truffle creations.

2 CUPS (250 G)

EQUIPMENT: *A baking sheet.*

2 cups (250 g) walnut halves

1 tablespoon tamari or other Japanese soy sauce

2 teaspoons Homemade Curry Powder (page 188)

1. Center a rack in the oven. Preheat the oven to 350°F (180°C).

2. In a bowl, combine the walnuts and tamari, tossing to coat the nuts evenly. Add the curry powder and toss once more. Spread the nuts in a single layer on the baking sheet.

3. Place the baking sheet in the oven and toast the nuts, shaking the sheet from time to time, until they are fragrant and toasted, 8 to 10 minutes. Remove from the oven and transfer the nuts to a dish to cool. (Store in an airtight container at room temperature for up to 1 month.)

TÊTE DE MOINE

Tête de Moine—which translates as "monk's head"—is a firm Swiss raw cow's milk cheese, sold in drums weighing about 1 1/2 pounds (750 g). It's a strong cheese, in flavor as well as aroma. Traditionally the cheese is shaved into thin ruffles with a gadget called a *girolle*: the drum of cheese is held in place by a stainless steel rod that juts up out of the center of a round cheese board. A horizontal blade with a handle is placed atop the cheese, and as the handle is turned, the knife cuts off elegant golden ruffles for your cheese tray.

Today Tête de Moine is made in just nine dairies. Its history dates from 1192, when monks in the monastery of Bellelay paid their rent on various properties with cheese made in their abbey. There are various stories as to the history of the name. One version suggests the nickname comes from the comparison between the shavings of the cheese and a monk's tonsure. Another story says the number of cheeses traditionally stored in the abbey was counted per the number of monks—or monk's heads—resident in the abbey.

"Acorns or oak trees
that are planted on the fifth day
of the new moon will produce
truffles five years later."

PASTA, RICE, AND GRAINS

GOAT CHEESE CANNELLONI WITH MORELS AND TRUFFLES 114

SPAGHETTI WITH PARMESAN AND TRUFFLE BUTTER 119

TRUFFLE RISOTTO WITH PARMESAN BROTH 121

TAGLIATELLE WITH FOIE GRAS, MORELS, AND TRUFFLES:
MACARONADE 125

TRENNE PASTA WITH JERUSALEM ARTICHOKES,
PARMESAN, AND TRUFFLES 128

MOREL MUSHROOMS, CHESTNUTS, FARFALLE,
AND TRUFFLE SALT 132

CÈPES WITH FRESH FETTUCCINE AND TRUFFLE BUTTER 134

SPAGHETTI CARBONARA WITH TRUFFLES 136

ÉPEAUTRE "RISOTTO" WITH MINCED TRUFFLES 138

GOAT CHEESE CANNELLONI WITH MORELS AND TRUFFLES

This pasta creation is hugely popular in our home. It is an updated version of one I sampled years ago in the dining room of the Hotel Lancaster in Paris. Here I've kept the same dreamy goat's milk cheese filling, but now I serve it topped with my "all-purpose" truffle sauce and morel mushrooms. It's a good dish for entertaining, for both the pasta and the sauce can be prepared several hours in advance and heated for just 20 minutes before serving. The recipe is long and may look daunting, but it is not complicated. And once you've prepared it, you will come back to this, as I do, time and again.

4 SERVINGS

EQUIPMENT: *Dampened cheesecloth; a 10-quart (10 l) pasta pot fitted with a colander; four 6-inch (15 cm) porcelain gratin dishes; a baking sheet.*

6 ounces (180 g) fresh goat's milk cheese

2 large ultra-fresh eggs, preferably organic and free range, at room temperature, lightly beaten (see Note)

Grated zest of 2 lemons, preferably organic

Fine sea salt

1 1/2 ounces (45 g) dried morel mushrooms

A 12-inch (30 cm) square sheet of fresh pasta (about 2 1/2 ounces; 75 g)

3 tablespoons coarse sea salt

1/2 cup (50 g) freshly grated Parmigiano-Reggiano cheese

About 1/2 cup (125 ml) Truffle, Morel, and Cream Sauce (page 192; see step 2)

1 fresh black truffle (about 1 ounce; 30 g each), cleaned (see Note, page 26)

1. Place the cheese on a large plate. Cover it with the eggs and lemon zest. Mash with a fork until the mixture has a thick, smooth consistency. Taste for seasoning. (The filling can be prepared up to 4 hours in advance, covered, and refrigerated.)

2. Place the morels in a colander and rinse well under cold running water to rid them of any grit. Transfer them to a heatproof 1-quart (1 l) measuring cup or bowl. Pour 2 cups (500 ml) of the hottest possible tap water over the mushrooms. Set aside for 20 minutes to plump them up.

3. Meanwhile, arrange a rack in the center of the oven. Preheat the oven to 350°F (180°C).

4. With a slotted spoon, carefully remove the mushrooms from the liquid, leaving behind any grit that may have fallen to the bottom.

5. Place the dampened cheesecloth in a colander set over a large bowl. Carefully spoon the morel soaking liquid into the colander, leaving behind any grit at the bottom of the measuring cup. (The liquid can be used to prepare the Truffle, Morel, and Cream Sauce.)

6. Prepare a large bowl of ice water. Arrange 3 large kitchen towels on the counter, for draining the pasta.

7. Cut the sheet of pasta into sixteen 3-inch (7.5 cm) squares.

8. Fill the pasta pot with 8 quarts (8 l) of water and bring it to a rolling boil over high heat. Add the coarse salt. Drop in as many squares of pasta as will comfortably float in the water. Cook for about 30 seconds, removing the squares with a slotted spoon while still very al dente. Transfer them to the ice water. Once all the squares are cooked, swish them around in the ice water, then transfer them with a slotted spoon to the kitchen towels, arranging them in a single layer.

9. Place the gratin dishes side by side on the baking sheet.

10. Lift a square of pasta off the towel and turn it over. (This helps ensure that the pasta does not stick to the towel as the cannelloni are prepared.) With a small spoon, spread about 2 teaspoons of the filling evenly along the bottom third of the square. Do not fill all the way to the edges, or the filling may leak. Carefully roll the pasta—jelly-roll fashion—into a cylinder and place it in a gratin dish, seam side down. Prepare the remaining cannelloni, arranging 4 rolled cannelloni side by side in each gratin dish. Sprinkle with the cheese.

11. Cover each gratin dish securely with foil, to prevent the pasta from drying out as it cooks. Place the baking sheet in the oven and cook until the cannelloni are bubbling, about 20 minutes.

12. While the pasta cooks, prepare the truffle. With a vegetable peeler, peel the truffle. Mince the truffle peelings for another use. Cut the truffle into thick slices, then into matchsticks.

13. Remove from the oven, remove the foil, and garnish each serving with the morels and several tablespoons of the sauce. Garnish with truffle matchsticks. Serve.

NOTE: *To infuse the eggs with truffle aroma and flavor, store a whole fresh truffle and the eggs (in their shells) in an airtight container in the refrigerator for at least 2 days and up to 1 week.*

WINE SUGGESTION: *One festive evening in June, we hosted a dinner party on the night of a full moon, dining beneath the pergola in the garden. In celebration of friendship, the brilliant setting sun, and the golden rising moon, I chose a decade-old white Châteauneuf-du-Pâpe from the Clos du Caillou vineyard. It was liquid gold, a fittingly elegant, crisp, acidic, mushroom-friendly wine.*

SPAGHETTI WITH PARMESAN AND TRUFFLE BUTTER

I'll come right out and say it: this is the easiest, best-value recipe in the book. How can you miss with a great bowl of spaghetti, a touch of truffle butter, freshly grated Parmigiano-Reggiano, and a sprinkling of truffle salt? If you have some minced truffle shavings, that would be great too, but even without them this dish offers some of life's simplest pleasures.

4 SERVINGS

EQUIPMENT: *A 10-quart (10 l) pasta pot fitted with a colander; 4 warmed shallow soup bowls.*

3 tablespoons coarse sea salt

1 pound (500 g) Italian spaghetti

2 tablespoons (1 ounce, 30 g) Truffle Butter (page 191)

1 cup (100 g) freshly grated Parmigiano-Reggiano cheese, plus additional for serving

Truffle Salt (page 186)

1 tablespoon (6 g) minced fresh black truffle or minced truffle peelings (optional)

1. Fill the pasta pot with 8 quarts (8 l) of water and bring it to a rolling boil over high heat. Add the coarse salt and the pasta. Cook until tender but firm to the bite. Drain thoroughly.

2. Transfer the pasta to a large bowl, add the butter and cheese, and toss to coat the pasta evenly and thoroughly. Season lightly with the truffle salt. Transfer to the warmed bowls, shower with minced truffle, if using, and serve. Pass the additional cheese.

WINE SUGGESTION: *This calls for an everyday red, and of course our favorite is our own Clos Chanteduc, a simple Côtes-du-Rhône, but one that forces you to sit up and take notice, focusing on its note of coarsely ground black pepper, the fine balance of fruit and acidity, as well as its easy-quaffing qualities. The blend of Grenache, Syrah, and Mourvèdre comes from vines planted mostly in the 1950s, so the flavors are rich and dense.*

"One does not reap if one plants; one reaps if one takes good care of plants."

American author Diane Ackerman compares the scent of the truffle to "the muskiness of a rumpled bed after an afternoon of love in the tropics" in her book *A Natural History of the Senses* (1990).

TRUFFLE RISOTTO WITH PARMESAN BROTH

Nothing satisfies like a warm bowl of perfectly cooked risotto. And when it is laced with truffles and cheese, you're on your way to heaven. We use a good deal of Parmigiano-Reggiano in our house, so our freezer is always full of tasty rinds for making Parmesan broth, which can also be frozen so the broth is always at hand. This dish deserves a very special white wine.

8 SERVINGS

EQUIPMENT: *Two small jars with lids; a mandoline or a very sharp knife; 8 warmed shallow soup bowls.*

PARMESAN BROTH

About 6 ounces (180 g) Parmesan rinds

RICE

2 fresh black truffles (about 1 ounce; 30 g each), cleaned (see Note, page 26)

2 tablespoons extra-virgin olive oil

2 plump, moist garlic cloves, peeled, halved, green germ removed, and minced

2 shallots, trimmed, peeled, and finely minced

Fine sea salt

2 cups (390 g) Italian Arborio rice

1 cup (100 g) freshly grated Parmigiano-Reggiano cheese, plus additional for serving

1. In a large saucepan, combine the Parmesan rinds and 6 cups (1.5 l) water. Simmer, stirring regularly to prevent the cheese from sticking to the pan, until the rinds are

very soft and the broth is fragrant, about 30 minutes. Strain the broth, discarding the rinds. Return the broth to the heat and keep it simmering, at barely a whisper.

2. With a vegetable peeler, peel the truffles. Mince the truffle peelings, place them in a jar, and tighten the lid. With the mandoline or very sharp knife, cut the truffles into very thin slices. Place the slices in a jar, and tighten the lid.

3. In another large saucepan, combine the oil, garlic, shallots, and salt, and sweat—cook, covered, over low heat without coloring until soft and translucent—3 to 4 minutes. Add the rice, and stir until it is well coated with the fats, glistening, and semi-translucent, 1 to 2 minutes. (This step is important for good risotto: the heat and fat will help separate the grains of rice, ensuring a creamy consistency in the end.)

4. When the rice glistens, add a ladleful of the simmering broth. Cook, stirring constantly, until the rice has absorbed most of the stock, 1 to 2 minutes. Add another ladleful of the stock, and stir regularly until all the stock is absorbed. Adjust the heat as necessary to maintain a gentle simmer. The rice should cook slowly and should always be covered with a veil of stock. Continue adding ladlefuls of stock, stirring frequently and tasting regularly, until the rice is almost tender but still firm to the bite, about 17 minutes total. The risotto should have a creamy, porridge-like consistency. Stir in the minced truffles and half of the cheese. Taste for seasoning.

5. Transfer the risotto to the warmed bowls. Garnish with the truffle slices and the remaining cheese. Serve immediately.

WINE SUGGESTION: *For this dish, I dig deep into my wine cellar, emerging with a two- or three-year-old bottle of white Châteauneuf-du-Pâpe, perhaps from one of the region's young new winemakers, such as Domaine Giraud or Domaine de Cristia. Marie and François Giraud's Les Gallimardes offers purity and freshness, with loads of my favorite Roussanne grape in the blend. At Cristia, Dominique and Baptiste Grangeon have created a flinty, flowery treasure.*

When a Parisian hostess asked food writer Maurice Edmond Sailland (1872–1956—better known by his pen name, Curnonsky, and dubbed the Prince of Gastronomy) how he liked his truffles, he replied, "In great quantity, madame, in great quantity."

TAGLIATELLE WITH FOIE GRAS, MORELS, AND TRUFFLES: *MACARONADE*

While researching *The Food Lover's Guide to France* in the mid-1980s, I sampled this dish often, with great relish, in a series of homes and restaurants in the country's southwest. A blend of fresh pasta, foie gras, wild as well as cultivated mushrooms, and of course a shower of truffles, it is a fitting regional dish that shows off the Périgord's culinary treasures.

4 SERVINGS

EQUIPMENT: *Two small jars with lids; a mandoline or a very sharp knife; dampened cheesecloth; a 5-quart (5 l) pasta pot fitted with a colander; 4 warmed shallow soup bowls.*

2 fresh black truffles (about 1 ounce; 30 g each), cleaned (see Note, page 26)

1 1/2 ounces (45 g; about 1 cup) dried morel mushrooms

1 cup (250 ml) Truffle Cream (page 189) or crème fraîche

1 teaspoon freshly squeezed lemon juice

Fine sea salt

Coarse, freshly ground black pepper

1 shallot, trimmed, peeled, and minced

2 tablespoons (1 ounce; 30 g) Truffle Butter (page 191) or salted butter

1 pound (500 g) fresh cultivated mushrooms, rinsed, trimmed, and thinly sliced

3 tablespoons coarse sea salt

10 ounces (300 g) fresh tagliatelle or fettuccine pasta

Truffle Salt (page 186)

4 ounces (120 g) fresh duck foie gras, cut into small cubes

1. With a vegetable peeler, peel the truffles. Mince the truffle peelings, place them in a jar, and tighten the lid. Reserve the peelings for another use. With the mandoline or very sharp knife, cut the truffle into thin slices. Place the slices in a jar, and tighten the lid.

2. Place the morels in a colander and rinse well under cold running water to rid them of any grit. Transfer them to a 1-quart (1 l) heatproof measuring cup or bowl. Pour 2 cups (500 ml) of the hottest possible tap water over the mushrooms. Set aside for 20 minutes to plump them up. With a slotted spoon, carefully remove the mushrooms from the liquid, leaving behind any grit that may have fallen to the bottom.

3. Place the dampened cheesecloth in a colander set over a large bowl. Carefully spoon the morel soaking liquid into the colander, leaving behind any grit at the bottom of the measuring cup. You should have 1 1/2 cups (375 ml) strained liquid.

4. In a large saucepan, combine the strained mushroom liquid and the truffle cream. Over high heat, reduce by half, 15 to 20 minutes. Season with the lemon juice and with fine sea salt and coarse pepper to taste.

5. In a large skillet, combine the shallots and butter and sweat—cook, covered, over moderate heat until soft and translucent—2 to 3 minutes. Add the cultivated mushrooms and sauté just until softened, about 5 minutes. Taste for seasoning. Add the morels and the cream sauce, and stir to blend. Cover and keep warm while you cook the pasta.

6. Fill the pasta pot with 3 quarts (3 l) of water and bring it to a rolling boil over high heat. Add the coarse salt and the pasta. Cook until tender. Drain thoroughly. Add the pasta directly to the skillet containing the mushrooms and sauce, tossing to coat it with the sauce. Cover and let rest for several minutes, for the pasta to absorb the

sauce. Mound in the warmed bowls. Season with truffle salt and garnish with the foie gras and truffle slices. Serve.

WINE SUGGESTION: *A new favorite white Châteauneuf-du-Pâpe comes from the vineyards of Château de la Gardine, where the Brunel family offers a special white cuvée, Cuvée des Générations Marie-Léoncie Vieilles Vignes, a saintly wine to be revered, a blend with 70 percent Roussanne from vines more than sixty years old.*

"That truffle seemed to me like earth and sky and sea. I felt at one with nature, that my mouth was filled with the taste of the earth. There was a ripeness, a naughtiness, something beyond description. A gastronomic black diamond, it was utter luxury and earthiness combined."

—PAULA WOLFERT, *THE COOKING OF SOUTHWEST FRANCE* (1983)

TRENNE PASTA WITH JERUSALEM ARTICHOKES, PARMESAN, AND TRUFFLES

In cooking, flavors often create such a strong bond of friendship that two plus two ends up tasting like twenty. Such is the case with this combination of Jerusalem artichoke soup turned into a puree, Parmigiano-Reggiano cheese, and of course, truffles. This is certainly an example of a poor man's root vegetable, such as the Jerusalem artichoke (also known as a sunchoke), serving as a perfect mate for the truffle. I created this dish over a Christmas we shared with friends Todd Murray and Douglas Sills. I confess that we savored the pasta more than once during that holiday!

4 SERVINGS

EQUIPMENT: *A 10-quart (10 l) pasta pot fitted with a colander; 4 warmed shallow soup bowls.*

3 tablespoons coarse sea salt

1 pound (500 g) Italian *trenne* pasta or penne pasta

3 cups (750 ml) reduced Jerusalem Artichoke Soup (page 74)

1 cup (100 g) freshly grated Parmigiano-Reggiano cheese, plus additional for serving

1/4 cup (25 g) minced fresh black truffles or minced truffle peelings

Truffle Salt (page 186)

1. Fill the pasta pot with 8 quarts (8 l) of water and bring it to a rolling boil over high heat. Add the coarse salt and the pasta. Cook until tender but firm to the bite. Drain thoroughly.

2. While the pasta is cooking, warm the reduced soup.

3. Transfer the pasta to a large bowl, and add the reduced soup, the cheese, and half of the minced truffles. Toss to coat the pasta evenly and thoroughly. Season lightly with the truffle salt. Transfer to the warmed bowls, shower with the remaining minced truffles, and serve, passing the additional cheese.

WINE SUGGESTION: *I adore the Italian wines from the Bonacossi family's Villa di Capezzana, where wine has been made for twelve centuries. Their well-priced Tenuta di Capezzana Barco Reale—a blend of Sangiovese, Cabernet, and Canaiolo grapes—is a fruity, earthy, mineral-rich red that loves pasta.*

A PROVENÇAL STORY: TRUFFLES AND HONESTY

Take five or six freshly dug truffles, and without brushing them, put them at the bottom of a large bowl big enough to fit a dozen eggs. Carefully place the eggs on top of the truffles without breaking them. Cover the bowl so it is airtight and place it in the refrigerator for a day or two.

When you have left the eggs for a day or two, make an omelet using your own method. The eggs will be wonderfully perfumed with the scent of truffles.

If you are honest, you will mix the eggs with the truffles, which you will have previously brushed under fresh water, peeled, and cut into small pieces.

If you are cheap, you will add only one or two truffles and supplement with pitted black olives cut very fine.

If you are dishonest, you won't add any truffles—just olives.

MOREL MUSHROOMS, CHESTNUTS, FARFALLE, AND TRUFFLE SALT

When creating this dish, I tried nearly a dozen different fresh and dried pastas—even deep brown soba noodles—and nothing seemed to find a home. Finally I hit on a variety of bowties, or farfalles, beautiful handmade specimens in beige and black, with about 10 percent of the pasta colored with squid ink. Their elegance matches that of the morels, the rich sauce, and the earthy chestnuts.

4 SERVINGS

EQUIPMENT: *Dampened cheesecloth; a 5-quart (5 l) pasta pot fitted with a colander; 4 warmed shallow soup bowls.*

1 1/2 ounces (45 g; about 1 cup) dried morel mushrooms

1 cup (250 ml) Truffle Cream (page 189) or crème fraîche

1 teaspoon freshly squeezed lemon juice

Fine sea salt

Coarse, freshly ground black pepper

1 shallot, trimmed, peeled, and minced

2 tablespoons (1 ounce; 30 g) Truffle Butter (page 191) or salted butter

3/4 cup (4 ounces; 120 g) cooked chestnuts

1 1/2 tablespoons coarse sea salt

8 ounces (250 g) dried Italian farfalle pasta

Truffle Salt (page 186)

1. Place the morels in a colander and rinse well under cold running water to rid them of any grit. Transfer them to a 1-quart (1 l) heatproof measuring cup or bowl. Pour

2 cups (500 ml) of the hottest possible tap water over the mushrooms. Set aside for 20 minutes to plump them up. With a slotted spoon, carefully remove the mushrooms from the liquid, leaving behind any grit that may have fallen to the bottom.

2. Place the dampened cheesecloth in a colander set over a large bowl. Carefully spoon the morel soaking liquid into the colander, leaving behind any grit at the bottom of the measuring cup. You should have 1 1/2 cups (375 ml) strained liquid.

3. In a large saucepan, combine the strained mushroom liquid and the truffle cream. Over high heat, reduce by half, 15 to 20 minutes. Season to taste with the lemon juice, and with fine sea salt and coarse pepper to taste.

4. In a large skillet, combine the shallots and butter and sweat—cook, covered, over moderate heat until soft and translucent—2 to 3 minutes. Add the mushrooms, chestnuts, and the cream sauce. Simmer gently for several minutes, to let the vegetables absorb the sauce. Taste for seasoning. Cover and keep warm while you cook the pasta.

5. Fill the pasta pot with 3 quarts (3 l) of water and bring it to a rolling boil over high heat. Add the coarse salt and the pasta. Cook until tender but still firm to the bite. Drain. Add the pasta directly to the skillet containing the mushrooms, tossing to coat it with the sauce. Mound in the warmed bowls. Garnish with the truffle salt, and serve.

WINE SUGGESTION: *A white Châteauneuf-du-Pâpe is in order here. I would go for one from Domaine de la Solitude, a wine that a sommelière once called "a red wine masquerading as a white," for it has so much depth and character.*

"Truffles are God's way of saying winter is okay!"

—STEVEN ROTHFELD, AMERICAN PHOTOGRAPHER

CÈPES WITH FRESH FETTUCCINE
AND TRUFFLE BUTTER

With a well-stocked pantry for the dried cèpes, a refrigerator for the cheese, and a freezer for the truffle butter and salt, I can play the hermit on the hill, not leaving my farmhouse in Provence for days on end. Even in the winter months my garden supplies me with fresh thyme and chives, so I am set. This makes a great main dish but is also a lovely side dish to roasted poultry.

4 SERVINGS

EQUIPMENT: *Dampened cheesecloth; a fine-mesh sieve; a 10-quart (10 l) pasta pot fitted with a colander.*

2 cups (40 g) dried cèpe mushrooms

2 tablespoons (1 ounce; 30 g) Truffle Butter (page 191)

2 tablespoons Truffle Cream (page 189) or heavy cream

3 tablespoons coarse sea salt

1 pound (500 g) fresh fettuccine pasta

1 cup (100 g) freshly grated Parmigiano-Reggiano cheese

3 tablespoons finely minced fresh chives

1/2 teaspoon fresh thyme, leaves only

Truffle Salt (page 186)

1. Place the mushrooms in a colander and rinse well under cold running water to rid them of any grit. Transfer them to a 1-quart (1 l) heatproof measuring cup or bowl. Pour 2 cups (500 ml) of the hottest possible tap water over the mushrooms. Set

aside for 20 minutes to plump them up. With a slotted spoon, carefully remove the mushrooms from the liquid, leaving behind any grit that might have fallen to the bottom.

2. Place the dampened cheesecloth in the sieve set over a large bowl. Carefully spoon the mushroom soaking liquid into the sieve, leaving behind any grit at the bottom of the measuring cup. You should have 1 1/2 cups (375 ml) strained liquid.

3. In a large saucepan over high heat, reduce the strained mushroom liquid to 1/2 cup (125 ml), about 10 minutes.

4. In a bowl that is large enough to hold the pasta, combine the mushrooms, the reduced mushroom liquid, the truffle butter, and the truffle cream.

5. Fill the pasta pot with 8 quarts (8 l) of water and bring it to a rolling boil over high heat. Add the coarse salt and the pasta. Cook until tender. Drain. Add the pasta to the bowl and toss to blend. Add the cheese, chives, and thyme, and toss once more. Season with the truffle salt. Serve.

WINE SUGGESTION: *Domaine de la Janasse in Châteauneuf-du-Pape makes a fine, well-priced Vin de Pays de la Principauté d'Orange, a 100 percent Viognier that nicely balances its floral qualities with a good level of acidity, making for a refreshing wine that I enjoy with pasta and mushrooms.*

SPAGHETTI CARBONARA WITH TRUFFLES

This classic spaghetti dish takes well to truffles, as well as to those fragrant, flavorful eggs that have inhaled the truffle's rich perfume.

4 SERVINGS

EQUIPMENT: *A small jar with a lid; a mandoline or a very sharp knife; a 10-quart (10 l) pasta pot fitted with a colander; 4 warmed shallow soup bowls.*

2 fresh black truffles (about 1 ounce; 30 g each), cleaned (see Note, page 26)

1 1/2 cups (5 ounces; 150 g) pancetta matchsticks

4 large ultra-fresh eggs, preferably organic and free range, at room temperature (see Note)

1/2 cup (50 g) freshly grated Parmigiano-Reggiano cheese

1/2 cup (35 g) freshly grated Pecorino-Romano cheese

3 tablespoons coarse sea salt

1 pound (500 g) Italian spaghetti

Truffle Salt (page 186)

Coarse, freshly ground black pepper

1. With a vegetable peeler, peel the truffles. Mince the truffle peelings, place them in the jar, and tighten the lid. Reserve the peelings for another use. With the mandoline or very sharp knife, cut one truffle into thin slices. Cut the second truffle into thick slices, then into matchsticks.

2. In a small dry skillet, brown the pancetta over medium heat until crisp and golden, about 5 minutes. With a slotted spoon, transfer the pancetta to several layers of paper

towels to absorb the fat. Blot the top of the pancetta with several layers of paper towels to absorb any additional fat.

3. In a shallow bowl that is large enough to hold all the pasta later on, mix the truffle slices and matchsticks, eggs, and both cheeses. (This can be done several hours in advance, letting the flavors blend. Store the mixture in an airtight container in the refrigerator until ready to use.)

4. Fill the pasta pot with 8 quarts (8 l) of water and bring it to a rolling boil over high heat. Add the coarse salt and the pasta. Cook until tender but still firm to the bite. Drain thoroughly. Add the pasta directly to the bowl containing the eggs, cheese, and truffles, tossing to coat it with the sauce. Add the pancetta and toss once more. Mound in the warmed bowls. Season lightly with the truffle salt and generous amounts of the pepper. Serve.

NOTE: *To infuse the eggs with truffle aroma and flavor, store a whole fresh truffle and the eggs (in their shells) in an airtight container in the refrigerator for at least 2 days and up to 1 week.*

WINE SUGGESTION: *When I consulted my friend Rolando Beramendi—expert in all things Italian—for a good wine pairing with this dish, he suggested a Barolo. My choice would be an elegant Aldo Clerico Barolo, full of spice, cherries, and raspberries.*

"The truffle has, too, an astonishing ability to transmit its perfume to other foodstuffs, seeping through the porous shells of fresh eggs when left alone with a basket full overnight; when slivered over a tangle of homemade pasta . . ."

—ELIZABETH LUARD, *TRUFFLES* (2006)

ÉPEAUTRE "RISOTTO" WITH MINCED TRUFFLES

In Provence, *épeautre* is known as "poor man's wheat," for it will grow in soil that is in-hospitable to most other crops. Its Latin name is *Triticum monococcum*. A firm, nutty grain, *épeautre*, or spelt, is so versatile that it can be used much like rice in risottos and salads, and it can be ground to a high-protein flour for making wholesome breads and pastries. Here I treat it like rice, cooking it in a fragrant bath of chicken stock and herbs, and finishing it off with a dose of truffle cream, truffle juice, and Parmigiano-Reggiano cheese. Serve this as a side dish to any roast poultry or meat dish, showered with a final, dramatic dusting of minced black truffles.

6 SERVINGS

EQUIPMENT: *A large fine-mesh sieve.*

3 cups (1 pound; 500 g) *épeautre* (spelt)

3 tablespoons extra-virgin olive oil

2 tablespoons (1 ounce; 30 g) unsalted butter

2 onions, peeled and minced

1 shallot, peeled and minced

Fine sea salt

About 5 cups (1.25 l) Homemade Chicken Stock (page 195)

2 imported bay leaves

1/2 cup (125 ml) Truffle Cream (page 189) or crème fraîche

1/2 cup (50 g) freshly grated Parmigiano-Reggiano cheese

1/4 cup (60 ml) truffle juice (optional)

2 tablespoons (12 g) minced fresh black truffles or minced truffle peelings

1. Pour the *épeautre* into the sieve and rinse it thoroughly. Transfer it to a large bowl, cover with cold water, and soak for 2 hours. (Soaking will help the grain cook more quickly.) Rinse again and drain.

2. In a large skillet, combine the oil, butter, onions, shallot, and a pinch of sea salt, and sweat—cook, covered, over low heat without coloring until soft and translucent— about 5 minutes. Add the *épeautre*, stock, bay leaves, and 1 teaspoon sea salt. Bring to a boil over high heat. Then reduce the heat to a simmer and cook, uncovered, until tender, about 20 minutes, stirring from time to time to keep the grain from sticking to the pan.

3. Place the sieve over a large bowl and drain the *épeautre* in the sieve, discarding the bay leaves and any remaining cooking liquid. Stir in the cream, cheese, and truffle juice, if using. Taste for seasoning. Sprinkle with the minced truffles.

WINE SUGGESTION: *Since the épeautre comes from the Ventoux, is makes sense to pair it with a wine from grapes grown nearby. I'd suggest a fine Côtes-du-Ventoux red, such as Domaine de Fondrèche Cuvée Nadal, a blend of Grenache, Syrah, and Mourvèdre grapes, all more than seventy years of age. It's a rich wine with spectacular freshness, one that will marry well with the creamy "risotto."*

"It was only September, however. There remained nearly two months before Saint Crespin, October 25, when the white truffle was said to turn gray, and a full two and a half months before Santo Margarido, November 16, when, with the first ground frosts, the gray truffle finally turned black. Then and only then could that mysterious fruit begin to be harvested."

—GUSTAF SOBIN, *THE FLY-TRUFFLER* (2001)

FISH, SHELLFISH, AND POULTRY

SIX-MINUTE STEAMED SALMON WITH
SHELLFISH CREAM AND TRUFFLES 142

WARM OYSTERS WITH TRUFFLE CREAM AND TRUFFLES 144

SEARED TRUFFLED SCALLOPS WITH COPPA AND
LAMB'S LETTUCE SALAD 147

SEARED DUCK BREAST WITH TRUFFLED *SAUCE POULETTE* 150

CHICKEN POT-AU-FEU WITH TRUFFLES 152

SIX-MINUTE STEAMED SALMON WITH SHELLFISH CREAM AND TRUFFLES

This is one of my all-time favorite truffle creations. It's a hit with my students, too. During a fall cooking week in Provence, we were blessed with the first-of-season shipment of Burgundy truffles and were able to savor this dish together. When we voted for "Best Taste of the Week" after the final feast, eight out of twelve students chose it as number one. The fattiness of salmon stands up well to the intensity of the truffle, and the soothing Truffle and Shellfish Cream adds a touch of elegance.

4 SERVINGS

EQUIPMENT: *Tweezers; a steamer; 4 warmed dinner plates.*

1 pound (500 g) salmon fillet, skin intact (see Note)

About 1 cup (250 ml) Truffle and Shellfish Cream (page 194)

A handful of fresh rosemary sprigs

Truffle Salt (page 186)

16 fresh black truffle slices

1. Run your fingers over the top of the salmon fillet to detect any tiny bones that might remain. With the tweezers, remove the bones. Cut the salmon into four 4-ounce (125 g) portions.

2. In a small saucepan, gently warm the shellfish cream.

3. Bring 1 quart (1 l) of water to a simmer in the bottom of a steamer. Place the rosemary on the steaming rack. Arrange the salmon fillets side by side, skin side down, on the rack. Season lightly with the salt. Place the rack over the simmering

water, cover, and steam just until the salmon flakes, about 6 minutes for medium-rare fish. Remove from the heat and let the fish rest for 2 to 3 minutes.

4. Carefully transfer the fish, still skin side down, to the dinner plates. Spoon the warm Truffle and Shellfish Cream over the salmon. Arrange 4 slices of truffle side by side over the cream on each serving. Serve.

NOTE: *The best choices are U.S. farmed (in tank systems) salmon (other market names: coho, silver salmon) or Alaskan wild-caught salmon (coho, chum [Keta], king, pink, red, silver, sockeye, sake).*

WINE SUGGESTION: *This dish deserves a knockout white. One that I never tire of is Domaine de la Mordorée's elegant Lirac Blanc, a complex blend of no fewer than seven grape varieties—Grenache Blanc, Viognier, Roussanne, Marsanne, Picpoul, Clairette, and Bourboulenc—each adding its own special note of fruit, acidity, aroma, and color.*

"It is the most capricious, the most revered of black princesses. It costs its weight in gold."

—COLETTE, *PRISONS AND PARADISE* (1932)

WARM OYSTERS WITH TRUFFLE CREAM AND TRUFFLES

The sauce for these brilliant, briny oysters is amazing and versatile. How could the combination of oyster liquor, cream, butter, and truffle juice be bad? The silken texture of the warmed oysters creates a fine contrast to the crunch of the truffle matchsticks.

4 SERVINGS

EQUIPMENT: *A fine-mesh sieve; a flat ovenproof serving dish; a small jar with a lid; a mandoline or a very sharp knife.*

12 large fresh oysters

1 cup (280 g) coarse sea salt

1 fresh black truffle (about 1 ounce; 30 g), cleaned (see Note, page 26)

1/4 cup (60 ml) Truffle Cream (page 189)

About 1 tablespoon truffle juice

2 teaspoons (10 g) Truffle Butter (page 191)

1/2 teaspoon freshly squeezed lemon juice, or to taste

1. Open the oysters, cut the muscle to extract each oyster from the shell, and filter the oyster liquor through the sieve set over a small saucepan.

2. Cover the bottom of the ovenproof serving dish (it should be large enough to hold the oysters in a single layer) with a thin layer of the coarse salt. Place the opened oysters, in their shells, on the bed of salt to keep them stable. Refrigerate. Within about 15 minutes, the oysters will give off a second, even more flavorful oyster liquor.

3. Meanwhile, arrange a rack in the oven about 5 inches (12.5 cm) from the heat source. Preheat the broiler.

4. With a vegetable peeler, peel the truffle. Mince the truffle peelings, place them in the jar, and tighten the lid. Reserve the peelings for another use. With the mandoline or very sharp knife, cut the truffle into thick slices. Cut the slices into matchsticks.

5. In the saucepan containing the reserved oyster liquor, add the cream and truffle juice and bring to a simmer over low heat. Whisk the butter and the lemon juice into the sauce, whisking vigorously to give it volume. If the sauce appears too thick, thin it with additional truffle juice. Add half of the truffle matchsticks and just warm them gently. Do not cook them.

6. Spoon the sauce over the oysters. Place the baking dish under the broiler and cook just until the oysters are warmed through, no more than 20 to 25 seconds. The sea-fresh aroma of oysters should begin filling the air as they warm up.

7. Cover 4 plates with the coarse sea salt to keep the oysters stable. Arrange 3 oysters on each plate. Garnish with the remaining truffle matchsticks. Serve.

WINE SUGGESTION: *With oysters, I always reach for a Picpoul de Pinet, a white that grows near the Mediterranean oyster beds. It is made with 100 percent Picpoul grape and has a distinct acidity and a pleasing spicy finish. Another great choice is always a Sauvignon Blanc, either a Sancerre or Quincy.*

When asked about the source of his inspiration, composer Gioacchino Rossini (1792–1868) said, "I am searching for motives and all that comes into my mind is pastries, truffles, and such things."

SEARED TRUFFLED SCALLOPS WITH COPPA AND LAMB'S LETTUCE SALAD

Somehow the sea-fresh, briny flavor of scallops loves the company of a faintly salty, smoky pork. Add a truffle and you've hit the jackpot! Shop around for a good pork product: I have settled on almost parchment-thin slices of Italian coppa, a dried and smoked style of pork that comes in slices just perfect for wrapping around half a scallop.

4 SERVINGS

EQUIPMENT: *A small jar with a lid; a mandoline or a very sharp knife; toothpicks; 4 large warmed dinner plates.*

2 fresh black truffles (about 1 ounce; 30 g each), cleaned (see Note, page 26)

SCALLOPS

8 large scallops (each 1 1/2 to 2 inches; 3 to 5 cm in diameter; see Note)

16 thin slices cured smoked pork, such as coppa, 2 1/2 x 3 1/2 inches (6.5 x 9 cm)

Coarse, freshly ground black pepper

SALAD

4 ounces (120 g) lamb's lettuce, rinsed, trimmed, and patted dry

Extra-virgin olive oil

Truffle Salt (page 186)

1. With a vegetable peeler, peel the truffles. Mince the truffle peelings, place them in the jar, and tighten the lid. Reserve the minced peelings for another use. With the mandoline or very sharp knife, slice the truffles into very thin rounds.

2. Gently pat the scallops dry with paper towels. Remove and discard the little muscle on the side of each scallop. Cut each scallop in half horizontally. Place several rounds of black truffle on top of each scallop. Wrap each scallop with a slice of coppa, and secure it with a toothpick. Set aside.

3. In a large skillet over moderate heat, sear the wrapped scallops, cooking just until the coppa is lightly browned, about 2 minutes on each side. Transfer to a double thickness of paper towels and season generously with the pepper.

4. In a large bowl, gently toss the lamb's lettuce with just enough oil to evenly coat the greens. Season with the salt.

5. Arrange 4 scallops on the side of each plate. Arrange a mound of salad alongside. Sprinkle the dressed salad with the remaining truffle slices. Serve.

NOTE: *The best choice is farmed bay scallops.*

WINE SUGGESTION: *This is the time to take out a great bottle of wine. My choice would be a white Châteauneuf-du-Pâpe, preferably a well-aged offering from Château La Nerthe, their special cuvée Clos de Beauvenir, a blend of 60 percent Roussanne and 40 percent Clairette. This showstopper has a perfect balance of fruit and acidity and forward, floral flavors that marry perfectly with the sweet, salty, smoky character of the seared scallops.*

"The most learned men have been questioned as to the nature of this tuber, and after 2,000 years of argument and discussion their answer is the same as it was on the first day: we do not know. The truffles themselves have been interrogated, and have answered simply: eat us and praise the Lord."

—ALEXANDER DUMAS, *GRAND DICTIONNAIRE DE CUISINE* (1873)

SEARED DUCK BREAST WITH TRUFFLED
SAUCE POULETTE

Eyes always light up when guests hear that *magret*, or fatted duck breast, is on the menu. It is a celebratory piece of poultry, one that is rich and satisfying. I like to serve this with a simple Truffled *Sauce Poulette*, preferably prepared with eggs that have had time to absorb the truffle's heady aroma.

4 SERVINGS

EQUIPMENT: *A warmed platter; 4 warmed dinner plates.*

2 fatted duck breasts (*magret*), each about 1 pound (500 g)

Fine sea salt

Coarse, freshly ground black pepper

1 cup (250 ml) Truffled *Sauce Poulette* (page 193)

Minced fresh black truffles, truffle slices, or minced truffle peelings, as the budget allows

1. Remove the duck from the refrigerator 10 minutes before cooking. With a sharp knife, make 12 diagonal incisions in the skin of each duck breast. Creating a crisscross pattern, make 12 additional diagonal incisions in the skin. The cuts should be deep but should not go all the way through to the flesh. (The scoring will help the fat melt while cooking and will stop the duck breast from shrinking up as it cooks.) Sprinkle the breasts all over with the salt and pepper.

2. Heat a dry skillet over medium heat. When the pan is warm, but not hot and smoking, place the duck breasts, skin side down, in the pan. Reduce the heat to low

and cook gently until the skin is a uniform deep golden brown, about 7 minutes. Using tongs, flip the breasts and cook skin side up for 7 more minutes.

3. Remove the duck breasts from the pan and place them side by side on the warmed platter. Season the meat generously with salt and pepper. Tent the platter loosely with foil and let the duck rest for at least 10 minutes, to let the juices retreat back into the meat.

4. In a small saucepan, heat the sauce.

5. To serve, slice the duck breasts on the diagonal into thick slices, and arrange them on the dinner plates. Spoon the sauce over the duck. Shower with the minced truffles or truffle slices. Serve.

WINE SUGGESTION: *The faintly bloody flavor of rich magret de canard demands an equally "wild" wine, which makes me think of the racy Gigondas from Domaine La Bouïssière, with gobs of cherry and black fruit flavor, a winning partner for the gamey duck.*

Beaucoup de pluie en juillet et août, beaucoup de truffes.
Lots of rain in July and August, lots of truffles.

—PROVERB

CHICKEN POT-AU-FEU WITH TRUFFLES

As this light, flavorful winter dish cooks, it fills the kitchen with warming, welcoming aromas and stimulates the appetite. It is a cold-weather Sunday night favorite, enjoyed as we sit by the fire and listen to our favorite music. Buy the best farm chicken you can find, as well as super-fresh vegetables. Whisking "truffled" eggs into the stock at the end is a nice enriching detail.

4 SERVINGS

EQUIPMENT: *Two small jars with lids; a large ovenproof casserole; 4 warmed shallow soup bowls.*

2 fresh black truffles (about 1 ounce; 30 g each), cleaned (see Note, page 26)

1 best-quality farm chicken (about 5 pounds; 2.5 kg), preferably organic and free range

Fine sea salt

Coarse, freshly ground black pepper

A handful of celery leaves

2 imported bay leaves

2 tablespoons freshly squeezed lemon juice, preferably organic

2 quarts (2 l) Homemade Chicken Stock (page 195)

8 carrots, peeled and cut lengthwise into thin strips

4 small leeks, white parts only, trimmed, cleaned, and cut into thick rounds

4 small turnips, trimmed, peeled, and cut crosswise into thick slices

2 large ultra-fresh eggs, preferably organic and free range, at room temperature (see Note)

Young fresh celery leaves, torn into bite-sized pieces, for garnish

Truffle Salt (page 186)

1. With a vegetable peeler, peel the truffles. Mince the truffle peelings, place them in a jar, and tighten the lid. Reserve the peelings for another use. With a knife, cut the truffles into chunks. Place the chunks in a jar, and tighten the lid.

2. Adjust a rack in the bottom of the oven. Preheat the oven to 375°F (190°C).

3. Liberally season the chicken inside and out with the salt and pepper. Stuff it with the celery leaves and bay leaves. Truss. Place the chicken in the casserole. Pour the lemon juice over the chicken. Add the stock to the casserole.

4. Place the casserole over moderate heat and bring the stock just to a simmer. Cover the casserole and place it in the oven. Cook for 25 minutes.

5. Add the carrots, leeks, and turnips to the casserole. Taste the stock for seasoning. Cover and return to the oven for another 25 minutes.

6. To serve, remove the chicken from the casserole and carve it into bite-sized pieces, cutting the breast meat into 1-inch-thick (2.5 cm) crosswise slices, then cubes. Transfer the chicken and the vegetables to a platter and keep it warm while you finish the sauce.

7. Whisk the eggs in a bowl. Gradually add a ladleful of the hot stock to the eggs, whisking constantly. Return the egg mixture to the stock in the casserole. Whisk again and bring the stock back to a simmer.

8. Place several pieces of chicken in each soup bowl. Arrange the vegetables around the chicken. Pour the egg-rich stock over the chicken and vegetables. Scatter with the celery leaves and truffle chunks. Season lightly with truffle salt.

NOTE: *To infuse the eggs with truffle aroma and flavor, store a whole fresh truffle and the eggs (in their shells) in an airtight container in the refrigerator for at least 2 days and up to 1 week.*

VARIATION: *The dish can also be served accompanied by a slice of toasted brioche slathered with foie gras and topped with truffle slices, as for the Sweet Onion Broth with Seared Foie Gras Toasts and Truffles (page 67).*

WINE SUGGESTION: *I enjoyed a version of this dish one January evening at our local bistro, Préface. It was the first time I sampled the white Côtes du Ventoux cuvée Quintessence from Château Pesquié. The blend of 80 percent Roussanne and 20 percent Clairette became an immediate favorite, a wine loaded with personality and a fine balance of fruit and acidity.*

"In Provence, spring arrives early. And that particular year it arrived even earlier than usual. Flowering almonds are its first, infallible sign. Their rosy petals seem to burst free of so much blank, desiccated wood, bringing with them—at that very same moment—a host of honeybees. Simultaneously, the air grows charged with the rich, ammoniacal scent of the blossoms themselves. Only days later, shrub after shrub of forsythia breaks into incandescent fire, and—just after that—japonica, too, in a rich profusion of pink coral-like droplets. Nature at that very moment of the year reasserts itself and sends up—one after another—its unmistakable signals. For Philippe Cabassac, however, this boded badly. It meant that soon, very soon, the truffle season would be coming to a close."

—GUSTAF SOBIN, *THE FLY-TRUFFLER* (2001)

VEGETABLES

TRUFFLES WRAPPED IN PARCHMENT AND WARMED
IN WOOD CINDERS 159

ZUCCHINI BLOSSOMS STUFFED WITH GOAT CHEESE
AND SUMMER TRUFFLES 161

TRUFFLE AND MOREL CLAFOUTIS 163

WILD MOREL MUSHROOMS STUFFED WITH DUXELLES 167

ONION AND GRUYÈRE GRATIN 170

TRUFFLES WRAPPED IN PARCHMENT AND WARMED IN WOOD CINDERS

This is one of the most dramatic truffle presentations I know. I first sampled it at Guy Jullien's restaurant La Beaugravière in Mondragon. While he usually wraps the whole truffle in pastry, I generally coat it with a bit of truffle butter and wrap it in parchment, then again in foil, securing it with household twine. Traditionally the preparation is warmed through in hot wood cinders in the fireplace. To serve, I remove the foil and place the truffle, still wrapped in parchment, atop a slice of buttered brioche. Guests are given a small scissors at the table to liberate the truffle from its wrapping, letting the juices and melted butter drip onto the brioche.

EQUIPMENT: *Baking parchment; household twine or raffia; warmed salad plates.*

FOR EACH SERVING

1 fresh black truffle (about 1 ounce; 30 g), cleaned (see Note, page 26)

2 teaspoons (10 g) Truffle Butter (page 191)

Fleur de sel

1 slice Brioche (page 178), toasted

1. Prepare a fire in advance. You will need sufficient hot wood cinders to bury the large wrapped truffles. (Alternatively, preheat the oven to 425°F/220°C.)

2. Prepare a 12 x 12-inch (30 x 30 cm) sheet of parchment paper. Fold the sheet of parchment in half. Place a truffle in the center of the folded piece of parchment. Generously coat all sides of the truffle with some of the truffle butter. Season lightly with the *fleur de sel*. Wrap the truffle like a beggar's purse, bringing the parchment up and around the truffle like a pouch. Tie securely with the household twine or raffia.

Prepare a 12 x 12-inch (30 x 30 cm) sheet of aluminum foil. Double-wrap the truffle in the same manner with the foil.

3.   Completely bury the wrapped truffle in the wood cinders. Or, fill a heatproof casserole with the hot ash, bury the wrapped truffle in the ash, and cover the casserole. (Alternatively, place the truffle on a baking sheet and place it in the center of the oven.) Heat the truffle until it is slightly softened but still crunchy and infused with the flavor of the butter and salt (*not* cooked through), about 10 minutes.

4.   To serve, brush the toasted brioche with the remaining truffle butter, and place it in the center of the warmed salad plate. Unwrap and discard the foil. Place the parchment-wrapped truffle on the center of the brioche. This will let the diner derive maximum pleasure from the juices that will flow from the truffle when the package is opened.

WINE SUGGESTION: *For this lavish preparation, pull out the best Champagne you can afford.*

"Those semi-mythical characters, the truffle agents, officiated each at his own table in the shade. One of them, quite tall and quite old, wore a monocle and used to say he kept in shape for the ladies by eating two or three truffles cooked in the ashes every morning."

—PIERRE MAGNAN, *DEATH IN THE TRUFFLE WOOD* (2006)

ZUCCHINI BLOSSOMS STUFFED WITH GOAT CHEESE AND SUMMER TRUFFLES

This summertime starter is as colorful as an August day, and just as welcome. I never tire of dreaming up uses for my morning harvest of golden zucchini blossoms, and this recipe puts the fragile, delicate flowers to perfect use. I mix best-quality fresh goat's milk cheese with my homemade truffle salt and summer truffle matchsticks and spoon the mixture into the blossoms. The blossoms are tied with a chive, then quickly steamed. The contrast of the soft cheese and the crunch of the fragrant truffle is mesmerizing. If you have a large double-decker Asian-style steamer, this is the time to put it to use.

4 SERVINGS

EQUIPMENT: *A small jar with a lid; a mandoline or a very sharp knife; a demitasse spoon; a steamer.*

1 fresh summer truffle (about 1 ounce; 30 g), cleaned (see Note, page 26)

8 ounces (250 g) fresh goat's milk cheese

1 large ultra-fresh egg yolk, preferably organic and free range, at room temperature (see Note)

Truffle Salt (page 186)

12 freshly picked zucchini blossoms

12 long, sturdy fresh chives

1. With a vegetable peeler, peel the truffle. Mince the truffle peelings, place them in the jar, and tighten the lid. Reserve the peelings for another use. With the mandoline or very sharp knife, cut the truffle into thick slices. Cut the slices into matchsticks.

2. Place the cheese on a large flat plate, and with a large fork, gently mash it. Add the egg yolk, and with the fork, gently mash the mixture. Sprinkle with the truffles and the truffle salt. Mash once more to evenly distribute the truffles and salt.

3. With the demitasse spoon, spoon the cheese mixture into each blossom. Carefully close each blossom, twisting to close. Wrap each one with a chive to hold the cheese in place. Bring 1 quart (1 l) of water to a simmer in the bottom of the steamer. Place the blossoms side by side on the steamer rack. Place the rack over the simmering water, cover, and steam just until the blossoms begin to wilt, just 1 to 2 minutes. Do not overcook. With a slotted spoon, transfer 3 blossoms to each of 4 salad plates. Garnish with the truffle salt. Serve.

NOTE: *To infuse the egg yolk with truffle aroma and flavor, store a whole fresh truffle and an egg (in its shell) in an airtight container in the refrigerator for 2 to 3 days.*

WINE SUGGESTION: *A summertime white such as the refreshing Côtes-du-Rhône Villages Rasteau blanc from Domaine des Escaravailles, a remarkably complex blend of some of my favorite white grapes, Roussanne, Marsanne, and Clairette.*

Ta femme, tes truffes, ton jardin, garde-les bien de ton voisin.

Your wife, your truffles, your garden, protect them from your neighbor.

—PÉRIGORDIAN PROVERB

TRUFFLE AND MOREL CLAFOUTIS

I love recipes in which substitutions are endless, and always with good results. This is one of them. Think of the clafoutis mixture of eggs, milk, cream, and nutmeg as a simple template. Many different fresh and dried, domestic as well as wild, mushrooms can be used. Both shiitake and chanterelle mushrooms are worthy, flavorful substitutes for the morels. The addition of thick matchstick slices of black truffles certainly gilds the lily.

6 SERVINGS

EQUIPMENT: *Dampened cheesecloth; six 1/2-cup (125 ml) ovenproof ramekins, egg coddlers, custard cups, tea cups, or* petits pots; *a roasting pan; a small jar with a lid; a mandoline or a very sharp knife.*

1 1/2 ounces (45 g; about 1 cup) dried morel mushrooms

3 tablespoons (1 1/2 ounces; 45 g) unsalted butter, plus extra for buttering the ramekins

1 shallot, peeled and finely minced

1/8 teaspoon fine sea salt

2 large ultra-fresh egg yolks plus 2 large ultra-fresh whole eggs, preferably organic and free range, at room temperature (see Note)

3/4 cup (185 ml) whole milk

3/4 cup (185 ml) Truffle Cream (page 189) or heavy cream

Freshly ground nutmeg

1 fresh black truffle (about 1 ounce; 30 g), cleaned (see Note, page 26)

1 tablespoon truffle juice (optional)

1. Place the morels in a colander and rinse well under cold running water to rid them of any grit. Transfer them to a 1 quart (1 l) heatproof measuring cup or bowl. Pour 2 cups (50 ml) of the hottest possible tap water over the mushrooms. Set aside for 20 minutes to plump them up. With a slotted spoon, carefully remove the mushrooms from the liquid, discarding any grit that may have fallen to the bottom.

2. Place the dampened cheesecloth in a colander set over a large bowl. Carefully spoon the morel soaking liquid into the colander, leaving behind any grit at the bottom of the measuring cup. You should have 1 1/2 cups (375 ml) strained liquid.

3. Center a rack in the oven. Preheat the oven to 350°F (180°C).

4. Lightly butter the ramekins and set them aside.

5. In a small skillet, combine the butter, shallots, and salt and sweat—cook, covered, over low heat until soft and translucent—about 3 minutes. Add the morels and cook until most of the liquid has evaporated, about 4 minutes. Spoon the morels into the ramekins.

6. In a large bowl, whisk together the egg yolks, whole eggs, milk, cream, and nutmeg. Pour the mixture over the morels and truffles. Fill the roasting pan with several inches of hot water and place the ramekins in the water bath. Place the roasting pan in the oven and bake until the puddings are firm and a knife inserted into the center of a clafoutis comes out clean, 35 to 40 minutes. The water should just simmer gently; check it halfway through the cooking time, and if necessary, add some boiling water.

7. While the clafoutis are baking, with a vegetable peeler, peel the truffle. Mince the truffle peelings, place them in the jar, and tighten the lid. Reserve the peelings to garnish the clafoutis once cooked. With the mandoline or very sharp knife, cut the

truffle into thick slices. Cut the slices into matchsticks. Place the matchsticks in a small bowl and cover with the truffle juice.

8.	Transfer each ramekin to a salad plate. Shower each one with the truffle slices and the juice, and the truffle peelings. Serve immediately.

NOTE: *To infuse the eggs with truffle aroma and flavor, store a whole fresh truffle and the eggs (in their shells) in an airtight container in the refrigerator for 2 to 3 days.*

VARIATION: *If you can find fresh morels, use 5 ounces (150 g) fresh mushrooms in place of the dried. Begin the preparation with Step 3.*

WINE SUGGESTION: *A recent Châteauneuf-du-Pâpe discovery for me is the red from the Mas de Boislauzon. Their wine is well priced, and a fine blend of 65 percent Grenache, 30 percent Mourvèdre, and 5 percent Syrah, a well-rounded wine with depth as well as freshness, a happy marriage with this vegetable clafoutis.*

"The following week, it snowed. The snow in itself, Cabassac recognized, was something altogether favorable, for it kept the truffle snug under its protective cover. Furthermore, the snow discouraged predators. For not only trufflers but boars, badgers, meadow mice, even those slow voracious snails—the *Helix promatea*—were drawn by the truffle's suave, subterranean perfumes. The snow, then, kept the truffle not only from man but from every other form of mammal, bird, gastropod."

—GUSTAF SOBIN, *THE FLY-TRUFFLER* (2001)

WILD MOREL MUSHROOMS STUFFED WITH DUXELLES

Throughout the fall and winter months, I prepare this fragrant vegetable dish frequently, serving it either as a main course or as a side dish to a golden roasted chicken. The cream sauce is particularly elegant with moist slices of chicken. For a lighter sauce, combine the mushroom soaking liquid with homemade chicken stock in place of the cream.

6 SERVINGS

EQUIPMENT: *Dampened cheesecloth; a small ovenproof gratin dish.*

MORELS

1 1/2 ounces (45 g) dried morel mushrooms

1 1/2 cups (375 ml) heavy cream or Homemade Chicken Stock (page 195)

1 tablespoon truffle juice

2 teaspoons freshly squeezed lemon juice, preferably organic, or to taste

Fine sea salt

Coarse, freshly ground black pepper

DUXELLES

1 tablespoon extra-virgin olive oil

1 shallot, peeled and finely minced

Fine sea salt

8 ounces (250 g) fresh mushrooms, rinsed, dried, and finely chopped

Several gratings of nutmeg

About 2 teaspoons freshly squeezed lemon juice

1 large ultra-fresh egg, preferably organic and free range, at room temperature (see Note)

Truffle Salt (page 186)

1. Place the morels in a colander and rinse well under cold running water to rid them of any grit. Transfer them to a 1-quart (1 l) heatproof measuring cup or bowl. Pour 2 cups (500 ml) of the hottest possible tap water over the mushrooms. Set aside for 20 minutes to plump them up.

2. While the morels are soaking, prepare the duxelles: In a large skillet, combine the oil, shallots, and a pinch of salt and sweat—cook, covered, over low heat until soft and translucent—about 3 minutes. Add the fresh mushrooms, nutmeg, and lemon juice. Cover and cook until the mushrooms are soft and cooked through, about 5 minutes. Stir in the egg to bind the mixture. Taste for seasoning. Set the duxelles aside.

3. With a slotted spoon, carefully remove the morels from the soaking liquid, leaving behind any grit that may have fallen to the bottom.

4. Place the dampened cheesecloth in a colander set over a large bowl. Carefully spoon the morel soaking liquid into the colander, leaving behind any grit at the bottom of the measuring cup. You should have 1 1/2 cups (375 ml) strained liquid.

5. In a large saucepan, combine the strained morel liquid and the cream or stock, and, uncovered, reduce by half over high heat, 15 to 20 minutes. Season with the truffle juice, lemon juice, and salt and pepper to taste.

6. Preheat the oven to 350°F (180°C).

7. Slit the morels down one side and open them up as flat as possible. With a demitasse spoon, fill the morels with the duxelles. Fold the mushrooms back to their original

shape. In the ovenproof gratin dish, arrange the stuffed morels side by side. Moisten with the reduced liquid. Cover the dish tightly with foil, and cook until bubbly and warmed through, about 15 minutes. Season with the truffle salt, and serve.

NOTE: *To infuse the egg with truffle aroma and flavor, store a whole fresh truffle and an egg (in its shell) in an airtight container in the refrigerator for at least 2 days and up to 1 week.*

"As is often the case, that late-summer thunderstorm was followed by an unabated blast of mistral. Often called the 'mudeater,' it dried even crackled the surface of the earth. Within a matter of days the topsoil grew as parched as a desert floor, Cabassac read this as a kind of signal. A geomorphic clue. Given the extent of the truffle's inordinate growth rate immediately following that late-summer thunderstorm, its rapid swelling blistered the surface of the earth a full twenty, thirty, even forty centimeters overhead. It left what is called a pèd-de-poulo or chicken-claw imprint upon the earth's surface. Cabassac knew exactly what to do at such times. Putting a handful of barley seeds in his pocket, he went out onto those abandoned terraces of his, following the line between the oak woods on one side, and the dead almond, cherry, and apricot orchards on the other. Whenever he came upon one of those pèd-de-poulo, he dropped barley seed into its very center, then moved on to the next."

—GUSTAF SOBIN, *THE FLY-TRUFFLER* (2001)

ONION AND GRUYÈRE GRATIN

Onions are seldom elevated to star status in the kitchen; rather they are relegated to understudy positions. Rarely do they get to show off all they can do, offering their elegant perfume and tender sweetness. This gratin welcomes the embellishment of a truffle-infused sauce, such as the Truffle and Shellfish Cream or Truffle, Morel, and Cream Sauce (page 142).

4 SERVINGS

EQUIPMENT: *Four 6-inch (15 cm) porcelain gratin dishes; a baking sheet.*

1 1/2 pounds (750 g) sweet white onions, peeled and cut crosswise into thin rings

3 tablespoons extra-virgin olive oil, plus more for oiling the gratin dishes

Fine sea salt

1/2 cup (2 ounces; 60 g) freshly grated Gruyère cheese

Several tablespoons Truffle and Shellfish Cream (page 194) or Truffle, Morel, and Cream Sauce (page 192)

1. Center a rack in the oven. Preheat the oven to 350°F (180°C).

2. In a large skillet, combine the onions, oil, and salt. Stir to coat the onions, and sweat—cook, covered, over low heat until soft and translucent—about 20 minutes. The onions should not brown.

3. Lightly oil the gratin dishes. Spoon the onions into the dishes. Sprinkle the onions with some of the cheese. Spoon 2 tablespoons of the Truffle and Shellfish Cream or the Truffle, Morel, and Cream Sauce over the onions. Sprinkle with the remaining cheese. Place the gratin dishes on the baking sheet. Place in the oven and bake until warmed through and golden, about 10 minutes.

*"Quand lo
pesseguier es en
flors / lo rabassier
es en plors."*

"Peach trees in
bloom / truffler's
doom."

—GUSTAF SOBIN,
THE FLY-TRUFFLER
(2001)

BREAD

PECORINO-ROMANO AND TRUFFLE PIZZA 174

BRIOCHE 178

THIN BREAD CRISPS 182

PECORINO-ROMANO AND TRUFFLE PIZZA

My good friend Serge Ghoukassian makes the most delicious truffle pizza at his charming restaurant, Chez Serge, in the center of the Provençal town of Carpentras. From June to August he serves up the fragrant pizza with fresh summer truffles; then from November to March the exalted winter truffle takes over. His version includes a healthy dose of olive oil and truffles scattered over the pizza once it has baked. I like to add a touch of cheese, and find that the peppery Italian Pecorino-Romano is perfect here. This dough makes a soft, chewy, puffy crust that is perfect for this simple pizza, but it can of course be used with more classic pizza toppings.

8 SERVINGS

EQUIPMENT: *A food processor; a baking stone; baking parchment; a pizza peel or baking sheet; two small jars with lids; a mandoline or a very sharp knife.*

3/4 cup (120 g) whole wheat flour

3/4 cup (120 g) bread flour

1 package (2 1/2 teaspoons; 5.5 g) instant yeast

3/4 teaspoon fine sea salt

1/4 teaspoon sugar

6 teaspoons extra-virgin olive oil, plus extra for brushing or spraying

1 cup (70 g) freshly grated Pecorino-Romano cheese

1 or 2 fresh black truffles (about 1 ounce; 30 g each), cleaned (see Note, page 26)

Truffle Salt (page 186)

1. In the food processor, combine the whole wheat flour, bread flour, yeast, sea salt, and sugar. Pulse to mix. Combine 1/2 cup (125 ml) warm water and 2 teaspoons of the oil in a measuring cup. With the motor running, gradually add enough of the water until the mixture forms a sticky ball. The dough should be soft. If it is too dry, add 1 to 2 tablespoons more hot water. If it is too sticky, add 1 to 2 tablespoons flour. Process until the dough forms a ball. Transfer to a clean, floured surface and knead by hand for 1 minute. Cover with a cloth and let rest for 10 to 20 minutes. (The dough will keep, covered and refrigerated, for up to 4 days; punch down the dough as it rises.)

2. About 30 minutes before baking, place the baking stone on the bottom rack of the oven. Preheat the oven to 500°F (260°C).

3. On a generously floured work surface, roll the dough into a 12-inch (30 cm) round.

4. Place a sheet of baking parchment on the pizza peel, and place the round of dough on the parchment. Brush the dough with 2 teaspoons of the oil.

5. Slide the dough off the peel and onto the baking stone (or the baking sheet, placing it on a rack in the oven). Bake for 5 minutes. Remove the pizza from the oven and sprinkle it with half of the cheese. Continue baking until the dough is crisp, golden, and puffy, about 5 minutes more.

6. While the pizza is baking, with a vegetable peeler, peel the truffle. Mince the truffle peelings, place them in a jar, and tighten the lid. Reserve the peelings for another use. With the mandoline or very sharp knife, cut the truffle into very thin slices. Place the slices in a jar, add the remaining 2 teaspoons oil, and tighten the lid. Shake to coat the truffles with the oil.

7. With the pizza peel, remove the pizza from the oven. Scatter the truffle slices on top. Brush or spray with olive oil. Season with truffle salt. Transfer to a cutting board and cut into 8 wedges. Serve immediately.

> **WINE SUGGESTION:** *For this elegant yet earthy pizza, I would go with a simple, daily drinking red. My choice would be Domaine de la Janasse's Vin de Pays de la Principauté d'Orange, cuvée Terre de Bussière, an atypical and solid Rhône Valley wine which contains 60 percent Merlot, along with Cabernet Sauvignon, Syrah, and Grenache.*

"The truffle is the most prestigious and perfumed of the mushrooms, with the unquestionable qualities of its aroma, a true black diamond of the kitchen. In the artist's palette of a chef, the truffle represents a touch of richness, of sumptuousness even. . . . It is to cuisine what embroidery is to sewing."

—RAYMOND OLIVER, FRENCH CHEF (1900–1990)

ON PECORINO-ROMANO

Beware—there is pecorino and there is pecorino. Pecorino-Romano is a prized Italian sheep's milk cheese made in Tuscany, Rome, and Sardinia. It is the sharp, spicy counterpart to Parmigiano-Reggiano and is used to grate over pastas and pizzas. It is one of Italy's protected cheeses, sporting the DOP (Denominazione di Origine Protetta, or Protected Designation of Origin) label. Cheese labeled simply "pecorino" can be any sheep's milk cheese made anywhere in Italy, found in many sizes and at many stages of aging.

INSTANT VS ACTIVE DRY YEAST

Many cooks are fearful of working with yeast, and now that there are so many options on the market, it can be even more intimidating. Here is how I use the various yeasts:

Instant yeast (also called rapid-rise, fast-rising, quick rise, bread machine yeast, pizza yeast) cuts the rising time in half, and I like to use it for recipes that are prepared at the last minute, such as this dough. This yeast is more finely granulated than active dry yeast and does not require warm liquid to be activated.

Active dry yeast is preferred when you want a long, slow rise that helps develop flavor in the dough. It has larger particle sizes than instant yeast, making it necessary to proof it—usually in warm water—before proceeding with a recipe.

BRIOCHE

I make this buttery brioche at least once a year, and always for our special truffle classes in January. It loves the company of a touch of truffle butter and truffles.

2 RECTANGULAR LOAVES

EQUIPMENT: *A heavy-duty mixer; two 4-cup (1 l) rectangular bread pans.*

SPONGE

1/3 cup (80 ml) whole milk, warmed

1 package (2 1/4 teaspoons; 5.5 g) active dry yeast

1 teaspoon sugar

1 large ultra-fresh egg, preferably organic and free range, at room temperature, lightly beaten

2 cups (280 g) unbleached, all-purpose flour

DOUGH

1/3 cup (65 g) sugar

1 teaspoon fine sea salt

4 large ultra-fresh eggs, preferably organic and free range, at room temperature, lightly beaten

1 1/2 cups (210 g) unbleached, all-purpose flour

12 tablespoons (6 ounces; 180 g) unsalted butter, at room temperature

Butter, for buttering the bread pans

1 large ultra-fresh egg, preferably organic and free range, at room temperature, beaten with 1 tablespoon cold water

1. *Prepare the sponge:* In the bowl of a heavy-duty mixer fitted with the dough hook, combine the milk, yeast, and sugar and stir to blend. Let stand until foamy, about 5 minutes. Then add the egg and 1 cup (140 g) of the flour, and stir to blend. The sponge will be sticky and fairly dry. Sprinkle with the remaining 1 cup (140 g) flour to cover the sponge. Set aside to rest, uncovered, for 30 to 40 minutes. The sponge should erupt slightly, cracking the flour.

2. *Prepare the dough:* Add the sugar, salt, eggs, and 1 cup (140 g) of the flour to the sponge. With the dough hook attached, mix at low speed for 1 or 2 minutes, just until the ingredients come together. Still mixing, sprinkle in the remaining 1/2 cup (70 g) flour. When the flour is incorporated, raise the mixer speed to medium and beat for 15 minutes, scraping down the hook and bowl as needed.

3. To incorporate the butter into the dough, it should be the same consistency as the dough. To prepare the butter, place it on a flat work surface and with a dough scraper, smear it bit by bit across the surface. When it is ready, the butter will be smooth, soft, and still cool—not warm, oily, or greasy.

4. With the mixer on medium-low speed, add the butter a few tablespoons at a time. When all of the butter has been added, raise the mixer speed to medium-high for 1 minute. Then reduce the speed to medium and beat the dough for 5 minutes. The dough will be soft and sticky.

5. First rise: Cover the bowl tightly with plastic wrap. Let the dough rise at room temperature until doubled in bulk, 2 to 2 1/2 hours.

6. Chilling and second rise: Punch down the dough. Cover the bowl tightly with plastic wrap and refrigerate the dough overnight, or for at least 4 hours, during which time it will continue to rise and may double in size again.

7. After the second rise, the dough is ready to use. If you are not going to use the dough immediately, deflate it, wrap it airtight, and store it in the freezer. The dough can remain frozen for up to 1 month. Thaw the dough, still wrapped, in the refrigerator overnight and use it directly from the refrigerator.

8. *To bake the brioche:* Butter the bread pans. Divide the dough into 12 equal pieces, each weighing about 2 1/2 ounces (75 g). Roll each piece of dough tightly into a ball and place 6 pieces side by side in each bread pan. Cover the pans with a clean cloth and let the dough rise at room temperature until doubled in bulk, 1 to 1 1/2 hours.

9. Center a rack in the oven. Preheat the oven to 375°F (190°C).

10. Lightly brush the dough with the egg wash. Working quickly, use the tip of a pair of sharp scissors to snip several crosses along the top of dough. (This will help the brioche rise evenly as it bakes.) Place the pans in the oven and bake until the loaves are deeply golden and an instant-read thermometer plunged into the center of the bread reads 200°F (100°C), 30 to 35 minutes. Remove the pans from the oven and place on a rack to cool. Turn the loaves out once they have cooled.

NOTE: *The brioche is best eaten the day it is baked. It can be stored for a day or two, tightly wrapped. To freeze, wrap it tightly and store for up to 1 month. Thaw, still wrapped, at room temperature.*

"Napoleon ate truffles before meeting Josephine in their amorous battles in the imperial bedchamber, in which it is no exaggeration to say, he always wound up defeated."

—ISABEL ALLENDE, *APHRODITE* (1997)

THIN BREAD CRISPS

Crunch is the operative word here. These little ultra-thin slices of bread are simply crisped in the oven and spread with truffle butter as a perfect accompaniment to eggs, salads, soup, or a cheese course.

I 2 CRISPS

EQUIPMENT: *A bread knife; a baking sheet.*

1 loaf sourdough bread

Extra-virgin olive oil spray

Truffle Butter (page 191)

1. Center a rack in the oven. Preheat the oven to 375°F (190°C).

2. With the bread knife, cut 12 ultra-thin slices from the loaf of bread. Arrange the slices side by side on the baking sheet (as many as will fit) and spray the bread lightly with the oil. Place in the oven and crisp until golden, about 10 minutes. Transfer them to a wire rack to cool, and repeat with the remaining slices.

3. Spread with the butter and serve immediately. (Store in a sealed plastic bag at room temperature for up to 3 days.)

THE PANTRY

TRUFFLE SALT

It was only a few seasons ago, after I went rather wild about creating all manner of seasoned salts, that I leapt with enthusiasm into the production of truffle salt. It's magic and is now one item that I am never without. Just the tiniest amount of minced truffle peelings paired with *fleur de sel,* or even with fine sea salt, can transform a dish—an effective way to extract the most out of the costly truffle. Even in the heat of summer, the salt is there in the freezer to perk up a salad, an egg dish, you name it. Don't embrace truffles without embracing truffle salt.

2 TABLESPOONS

EQUIPMENT: *A small jar with a lid.*

1 tablespoon (6 g) minced fresh black truffle peelings

1 tablespoon *fleur de sel* or fine sea salt

1. In the small jar, combine the minced truffles and salt. Tighten the lid and shake to blend. Refrigerate for up to 1 week or freeze for up to 1 year.

2. For each use, remove the truffle salt from the freezer or refrigerator, remove the desired amount, and return the jar to the freezer or refrigerator.

HOMEMADE CURRY POWDER

A trip to Vietnam inspired this homemade curry powder. The fragrance and power of the star anise and the intensity of the Vietnamese cassia cinnamon make all the difference here.

¹/₃ CUP (5 TABLESPOONS)

EQUIPMENT: *An electric spice grinder or a coffee mill; a small jar with a lid.*

2 small dried red chile peppers

4 pieces star anise

2 tablespoons whole coriander seeds

1 tablespoon whole cumin seeds

1 teaspoon black mustard seeds

1 teaspoon whole black peppercorns

1/2 teaspoon ground ginger

1/2 teaspoon ground turmeric

1/2 teaspoon Vietnamese cassia cinnamon

1/2 teaspoon ground fenugreek

1. In a small dry skillet, combine the chile peppers, star anise, coriander, cumin, mustard seeds, and peppercorns, and toast over medium heat, shaking the pan often to prevent burning, for 2 to 3 minutes.

2. Remove from the heat, and transfer to a plate to cool. In the spice grinder or coffee mill, grind to a fine powder.

3. Transfer the powder to the jar. Add the ginger, turmeric, cinnamon, and fenugreek. Tighten the lid and shake to blend. (Store in the jar at room temperature for up to 1 month.)

TRUFFLE CREAM

Truffle cream is a refrigerator staple come truffle season. The fat in the cream fixes the flavor of the truffle, infusing the cream with all of its finest qualities: earthy aroma and rich, intense flavors.

2 CUPS (500 ML)

EQUIPMENT: *A jar with a lid.*

5 tablespoons (1 ounce; 30 g) minced fresh black truffle peelings

2 cups (500 ml) heavy cream

In the jar, combine the truffles and cream. Cover securely and shake to blend. Refrigerate for at least 2 days before using. (The mixture will stay fresh, stored in an airtight container in the refrigerator, for 1 week.)

De Sainte-Croix (14 septembre) à Saint-Michel (24 septembre) la pluie ne reste pas au ciel; elle fait naître la truffe tardive, mais pour la faire belle, il est trop tard . . .

From Holy Cross Day (September 14) to Saint Michael's Day (September 24) the rain does not stay in the heavens; it gives birth to the late truffle, but for the truffle to be beautiful, it is already too late . . .

—PROVERB

TRUFFLE BUTTER

One needs only a few tablespoons of minced fresh truffles to create an all-purpose, fragrant butter, perfect for spreading on toast, melting into fresh pasta, or folding into a risotto. You can use the butter freshly made, or you can freeze it and use it throughout the year for added truffle pleasure.

4 TABLESPOONS (2 OUNCES; 60 G)

EQUIPMENT: *A small jar with a lid.*

1 tablespoon (6 g) minced fresh black truffle peelings

4 tablespoons (2 ounces; 60 g) salted butter, softened

1. Place the butter on a large plate. Sprinkle with the truffle peelings and mash with a fork to blend. Transfer to the jar. Tighten the lid.

2. Refrigerate for up to 3 days or freeze for up to 6 months. Serve at room temperature or melted, as necessary.

TRUFFLE, MOREL, AND CREAM SAUCE

It seems as though it took me forever to come up with an original truffle sauce I truly loved. Now I feel the wait was worth it: here it is, a mixture of the liquid reserved from plumping dried morel mushrooms, canned truffle juice, and heavy cream. I like the fact that it can be prepared any time of the year and is as versatile as it is perfumed and intensely flavored.

1 1/4 CUPS (310 ML)

EQUIPMENT: *A fine-mesh sieve.*

1 cup (250 ml) morel soaking liquid (page 116)

1/2 cup (125 ml) truffle juice

1 cup (250 ml) heavy cream

1. In a large saucepan, reduce the mushroom liquid, uncovered, over high heat by half, about 10 minutes.

2. Add the truffle juice and cream to the saucepan. Reduce, uncovered, over high heat by half, about 15 minutes.

3. Pour through the sieve into a bowl. (Store in an airtight container in the refrigerator for up to 3 days or in the freezer for up to 6 months.) Reheat at serving time.

VARIATION: *Replace the morel mushroom liquid with cèpe mushroom liquid.*

TRUFFLED *SAUCE POULETTE*

Sauce poulette is a simple, classic sauce, basically a roux—quickly cooked flour, fat, and liquid—to which one adds lemon juice, egg yolks, and a touch of cream. All the makings of a perfect truffle trilogy, prepared with truffle butter, truffle cream, and truffled eggs.

2 CUPS (500 ML)

3 tablespoons (1 1/2 ounces; 45 g) Truffle Butter (page 191)

1/4 cup (40 g) unbleached, all-purpose flour

1 2/3 cups (410 ml) Homemade Chicken Stock (page 195)

1 tablespoon freshly squeezed lemon juice, preferably organic

4 large ultra-fresh egg yolks, preferably organic and free range, at room temperature (see Note)

3 tablespoons Truffle Cream (page 189)

Truffle Salt (page 186)

1. In a saucepan, melt the truffle butter over low heat. Add the flour all at once, whisking to blend.

2. Add half the stock, whisking constantly. Add the remaining stock, whisking until the sauce is smooth.

3. Off the heat, whisk in the lemon juice, egg yolks, and truffle cream. Taste for seasoning, adding truffle salt if needed. The sauce can be prepared up to 1 hour in advance and reheated at serving time.

NOTE: *To infuse the egg yolks with truffle aroma and flavor, store a whole fresh truffle and the eggs (in their shells) in an airtight container in the refrigerator for at least 2 days and up to 1 week.*

TRUFFLE AND SHELLFISH CREAM

Shellfish broth is one of my secret weapons in the kitchen. I always feel it's a "free" ingredient, since I save up the well-rinsed shells of shrimp and langoustines and store them in the freezer until I have enough to make a fragrant broth, and then find all manner of uses for it. This is an intensely flavorful truffle sauce to spoon over fish or shellfish and top with a truffle garnish. I like to think of it as a lean sauce masquerading as a rich one, for it has an astonishing depth of flavor, with a great length, like a fine wine.

1 1/4 CUPS (310 ML)

EQUIPMENT: *A fine-mesh sieve.*

1/2 cup (125 ml) truffle juice

1 cup (250 ml) Shellfish Broth (page 65)

1 cup (250 ml) thick crème fraîche or heavy cream

1. Combine all the ingredients in a large saucepan and bring to a boil, uncovered, over high heat. Reduce by half, about 15 minutes.

2. Filter into a container through a fine-mesh sieve. (Store in an airtight container in the refrigerator for up to 1 day or in the freezer for up to 6 months.) Reheat at serving time.

HOMEMADE CHICKEN STOCK

A fine, rich, golden chicken stock forms the backbone of any kitchen and is an essential ingredient in every cook's "pantry." Leaving the peel on the onions helps give the broth its golden color, and scorching the onion halves over direct heat gives the final stock a rich, mildly smoky flavor.

3 QUARTS (3 L)

EQUIPMENT: *A long-handled 2-pronged fork; a 10-quart (10 l) pasta pot fitted with a colander; a fine-mesh skimmer; a wire mesh tea infuser or cheesecloth.*

2 large onions, halved crosswise (do not peel)

4 whole cloves

1 large farm-fresh chicken (about 5 pounds; 2.5 kg), preferably organic and free range

2 teaspoons coarse sea salt

4 carrots, scrubbed and cut crosswise into 1-inch (2.5 cm) pieces (do not peel)

1 plump, moist garlic head, halved crosswise (do not peel)

4 celery ribs

1 leek (white and tender green parts), halved lengthwise, cleaned, and cut crosswise into 1-inch (2.5 cm) pieces

One 1-inch (2.5 cm) piece of fresh ginger, peeled

12 whole black peppercorns

1 bouquet garni: several imported bay leaves, fresh celery leaves, thyme sprigs, and parsley sprigs, encased in a wire-mesh tea infuser or bound in a piece of cheesecloth

1. One at a time, spear each onion half with the fork and hold it directly over a gas flame (or directly on an electric burner) until scorched. Stick a clove into each of the scorched onion halves.

2. Place the chicken in the pasta pot and fill with 5 quarts (5 l) of cold water. Add the onions, salt, carrots, garlic, celery, leeks, ginger, peppercorns, and bouquet garni. Bring to a gentle simmer, uncovered, over moderate heat. Skim to remove any scum that rises to the surface. Add additional cold water to replace the water removed and continue skimming until the broth is clear. Simmer until the chicken is cooked, about 1 hour.

3. Remove the chicken from the pot. Remove the chicken meat from the carcass and reserve it for another use. Return the skin and the carcass to the pot and continue cooking at barely a simmer for another 2 1/2 hours.

4. Line a large colander with a double layer of dampened cheesecloth and place the colander over a large bowl. Ladle—do not pour—the liquid into the colander to strain off any impurities. Discard the solids. Measure. If the stock exceeds 3 quarts, return it to moderate heat and reduce. Transfer the stock to containers, and cover.

5. Immediately refrigerate the stock. When it is cold, spoon off all traces of fat that have risen to the surface. (Store the stock in airtight containers in the refrigerator for up to 3 days, or in the freezer for up to 3 months.)

VARIATION: *Use 2 whole cooked chicken carcasses rather than a whole raw chicken. The resulting stock will not have the same clean, fresh flavor, but it is worthy nonetheless. Or, use about 4 pounds (2 kg) of inexpensive raw chicken necks, wings, and backs to prepare the stock.*

TIPS FOR STOCK-MAKING

- For a clear stock, begin with cold water and bring it slowly to a simmer. Never let a stock boil or it will be cloudy, since the fat will emulsify. Cold water also aids in extracting greater flavor.

- For the first 30 minutes of cooking, skim off the impurities that rise to the surface as the stock simmers.

- Use a tall pot, for it will limit evaporation. I always use a large pasta pot fitted with a colander, which makes it easy to remove the solid ingredients and begin to filter the stock.

IS IT STOCK, BROTH, OR CONSOMMÉ?

Generally, a stock is cooked for a long time, up to 4 hours, while a broth—usually lighter—is cooked for a short time, typically around 40 minutes. A consommé is a stock that has been clarified, usually with egg whites. Sometimes stocks are also referred to as a bouillon, but ordinarily this term is used in reference to a court bouillon, usually of fish or vegetables.

Truffle Sources

PLANTIN AMERICA INC.
Weehawken, NJ
888-595-6214
www.plantin.com
Fresh, frozen, and canned black truffles;
Burgundy truffles; white truffles; truffle slicer.

D'ARTAGNAN
Newark, NJ
800-327-8246
www.dartagnan.com
Burgundy truffles; fresh black winter truffles.

OREGON WILD EDIBLES
Eugene, OR
541-484-0793
www.oregonwildedibles.com
Fresh Oregon black and white truffles, frozen year-round, fresh in season.

SABATINO TARTUFI
Bronx, NY
888-444-9971 or 718-328-4120
www.sabatinotartufi.com
Canned black truffles.

POLARICA
San Francisco, CA
800-426-3872
www.polaricausa.com
Fresh and canned truffles.

URBANI TRUFFLES
New York, NY
212-247-8800
www.urbanitrufflesonline.com
Fresh and preserved white and black truffles; fresh Burgundy truffles.

GOURMET FOODSTORE
Miami Gardens, FL
877-220-4181
www.gourmetfoodstore.com
Canned Burgundy truffles.

DEAN AND DELUCA
New York City and nationwide
800-221-7714
www.deandeluca.com
Fresh black truffles.

EARTHY DELIGHTS
DeWitt, MI
800-367-4709
www.earthy.com
Fresh black truffles.

At home with Patricia Wells Truffle Class 2010

Acknowledgments

This book would not exist without the longtime friendship of Hervé Poron of Plantin, our truffle supplier in Provence for more than twenty-five years. He has been a loyal friend, a great source of truffle inspiration and information, and a ready host and guest at our many truffle extravaganzas over the years. His son, Christopher Poron, and colleague Nicolas Rouhier have been equally important in our life in truffles and in Provence.

I must also thank all the truffle hunters and their adorable dogs, all of whom have enriched our lives over the decades of hunting winter black truffles in the sun, the rain, the pesky Mistral winds, the snow. Special thanks to truffle hunters Laurent, Bernard, Stephane, and Christian and their frisky dogs, Pamela, Dynamo, Lassie, and Come On.

Thank you, Jonathan Burnham, publisher of Harper, for saying yes to this idea the day I proposed it, and to my talented agent and friend Amanda Urban for being the first to believe in the project. At William Morrow my greatest thanks to editor Cassie Jones and her able assistant, Jessica Deputato. You helped make getting the book out a breeze! Thank you, designer Lorie Pagnozzi—you made such a beautiful and dreamy book! Also at William Morrow thanks to Liate Stehlik, Lynn Grady, Andy Dodds, Tavia Kowalchuk, and Shawn Nicholls. At home, a huge debt of gratitude and friendship to my assistant and good friend Emily Buchanan.

But nothing good would happen without my loving partner, Walter Wells, who brings joy to my life every waking moment.

—PATRICIA WELLS

INDEX

Note: Page references in *italics* indicate photographs.